D1245436

NO GRAIL WITHOUT DRAGONS

A Man's Unconventional Path to Love, Purpose, and Peace

Victor J. Giusfredi

NO GRAIL
WITHOUT DRAGONS

A Man's
Unconventional
Path to Love,
Purpose,
and Peace.

VICTOR J. GIUSFREDI

This memoir is aimed to inspire and offer insights into achieving a balanced state of well-being based on the experiences detailed within these pages. While it is believed that the principles presented herein can benefit readers, it is essential to emphasize that individual results may vary. The author and this literary work cannot be held liable for any outcomes that readers may experience as they apply these ideas to their own lives. It is sincerely hoped that readers approach this memoir with an open mind and understand that personal responsibility and discretion are essential in implementing any self-development strategies.

Published in 2023 by
Victor J. Giusfredi

Editor, Victor J. Giusfredi

Copyright @2023 Victor J. Giusfredi

Click or visit:
www.victorgiusfredi.com
hello@victorgiusfredi.com

Library of Congress Cataloging-in-Publication Data.
Giusfredi, Victor J.
        No grail without dragons: a man's unconventional path to love, purpose, and peace.
    ISBN:979-8-9883443-7-7(hardcover)
    ISBN:979-8-9883443-5-3 (paperback)
    ISBN:979-8-9883443-1-5 (eBook)

"Twenty years from now you will be more disappointed by the things that you didn't do than by the ones you did do. So throw off the bowlines. Sail away from the safe harbor. Catch the trade winds in your sails. Explore. Dream. Discover."
— Mark Twain

To my children, Isabella and Maximo:

You are the stars that guide me through life's darkest nights, the unwavering compass of my journey, and the infinite source of my love and inspiration.

To Aspen:

Thank you for making this book possible, enduring challenges together and nurturing our love through the storms. You've made this journey possible in ways I can never fully express.

And to every dreamer, seeker, and warrior who embarks on this narrow path:

May these words light your way, fortify your resolve, and lead you the boundless treasures of love, purpose, and peace. Don't stop seeking; the treasure you dream of awaits your discovery.

With love and gratitude,

Victor.

Introduction

After achieving every goal in my pursuit of happiness, I confronted a stark truth—I had failed. My life brimmed with diverse experiences: living and working in over 40 places, launching seven businesses and inventions, overcoming two marriages and divorces, learning the ropes of single parenting, and navigating a career path from janitorial work to international franchise owner — all by the age of 36. Yet, I hadn't found the combination for the emotional state I so ardently sought.

My quest for happiness encompassed different — yet intertwined — stages; pursuing sensory pleasures, avoiding pain by seeking gratification, and engaging in various forms of self-restraint. Yet no approach produced the state I intuitively sought; a balanced existence between reason and unreason, atheism and superstition, and the feeling of *knowing* things are ok in the middle of a storm.

And only the worst circumstances could push me to dive deeper, eventually stumbling upon the ingredients that contributed to the life I dreamed of; one where Love, Purpose and Peace aren't modern cliches, but worthy pursuits.

Within these pages lies the path and clues I encountered — a journey through the depths of my human experience, lessons culled from unexpected trials, and the wisdom that emerged from the shadows of my life. Through this book, I hope to help you sidestep common pitfalls and pain on your quest for happiness, by sharing the keys that turned my life around.

Join me as we unearth new paths to sustainable fulfillment and self-discovery. As you peruse the following chapters, you'll encounter windows into pivotal moments, raw emotions, and life's profound lessons that helped me discover a fountain of joy, happiness, and peace.

These 33 chapters resemble pieces of a complex puzzle; finding outer balance by delving into oneself. Jump in wherever your curiosity beckons and watch them seamlessly interweave to craft your unique narrative. While each chapter possesses individual significance, together, they form a map crafted from my diverse experiences around the world; map that I hope will lead you to the ultimate treasure.

In the forthcoming pages, we'll confront the dragons of fear, insecurity, and pain; the inner obstacles that safeguard the gate to your authentic self. I hope my book stands as your guide, your companion, and your mirror, helping you easily overcome the challenges to uncover the untapped potential within you.

To a life of Love, Purpose, and Peace.

Temet Nosce,

Victor J. Giusfredi

CONTENTS

I.

Midnight Revelation: Finding Hope in the Darkest Hour

"The world breaks everyone, and afterward, some are strong at the broken places."
- Ernest Hemingway, A Farewell to Arms

Love, Purpose, Peace. Three words that represented the meaning of my life, yet took over two decades to experience, and find.

From the time I turned 13, I had been on a relentless pursuit of something elusive, a feeling I couldn't explain but had stumbled upon before. I traveled the world in search of it, guided by intuition and the promise of love. However, this path led me to numerous failures and pain, as if crossing the street with my eyes closed.

Frustrated with my constant failures, I decided to address the areas in my life that I thought needed improvement; professional, physical well-being, and finances. I raced through life stages, hoping to find love and purpose, or at the very least, to feel good enough.

By the age of 25, I had experienced luxury, cars, women, and excess. My younger self had dreamed of such accomplishments. But divorced and nihilistic, I found myself lost and without direction. To deal with the pain, I sold everything I owned and vagabonded the world for two years, soul searching.

I certainly didn't need another adventure, but back then, it seemed like a good escape from my inner torment. From one quest to the next, I traveled the world looking for love, purpose, and peace.

After years of inner and outer battles, I had landed in Utopia; At

33, my dreams of a family, owning a business and working in Corporate America had all materialized. Little did I know that my life would take a drastic turn. In less than 18 months, I went from being a husband, a business owner, and a corporate worker to being unemployed, homeless, divorced, and broken.

I lived in my car for 3 months. Without credit or 3 months of rent no-one would take me in, and ended moving into the same place I moved out of when my ex-wife and daughter arrived. For the first few weeks, I sobbed at every patch on the wall, or crayon mark left by our previous life.

The month after moving in, I crash-landed into the role of mom and dad to my two kids, while wrestling with unemployment. To make ends meet, I sold my belongings, applied to jobs that paid half of what I earned before, and even swallowed my pride by asking my brother for money – something I had vowed never to do. I found myself at rock bottom physically, mentally, and emotionally.

In romantic relationships, breakups presented an opportunity for growth or a chance to find someone better suited for me. However, over 40 failed attempts at "making it work" and two divorces snatched my desire to try again. I tried to fix what others deemed bad about me, yet I failed to hit the mark every time.

Breakups became my most dreaded situations. How could it be that no-one wanted to stay with me? What had I done to attract infidelity, neglect, and even aggression from my partners, friends, and family?

What was wrong with me?

Throughout my life, many considered me not worthy of their affection, approval, or support. A few others even made it clear that life would be better without me in it. People I loved cursed the day they met me, and even my biological father, who abandoned my mother and me during her pregnancy, didn't bother to acknowledge my existence, calls or emails once I found him.

My desperate attempts at grasping significance or certainty had pushed me to the edge of the abyss. No adventure, achievement or emotional connection had led me to love or peace, and my purpose eluded me as I ran out of things to embark on.

Life became meaningless and the burden of my failures tormented me. Although I fantasized about what life would be like without such pressures, my children needed me more than anyone, and I had to get myself back together.

For months I dug into the archives of my memory to look for clues and answers to ease my pain. In the past, I had stumbled upon turning difficult situations into opportunities, simply by changing my mental perspective and perception of them. Intuitively, I knew that exposing my erratic behavior would lead to better outcomes, and better outcomes were exactly what I needed.

My kids were stressed and confused amid divorce and chaos, I drowned in financial debt, and hundreds of job applications resulted in nothing. Lost in confusion, I envisioned sparing my children from countless problems with the money from my personal life insurance policy. They hadn't asked for any of this, nor had they done anything wrong. Yet, they suffered due to my decisions and shortsightedness.

Convinced that the world would be better off without me, I sat on the couch past midnight, conjuring reasons to stay alive. To make this choice, I reflected on my past and wondered if any of the pain I had endured had been for anything. Did I have to keep fighting the current to end up shipwrecked? My body sank into the couch as resignation washed over me, realizing I had no desire to go on.

I buried my face in my hands, sobbing in a mix of regret, repentance, and desperation. My breathing shortened, causing my hands and legs to tremble while I tried to rescue myself from this swarm of negative emotions. Nausea distorted my self-awareness while I came to terms with my Fate.

I closed my eyes and asked my children for forgiveness – forgiveness for failing as a father, a husband, and a man. The weight of every mistake sunk me to a bottomless pit, where the beast of regret awaited to finish me.

Within an instant, I accepted death in every realm, and simultaneously, found my purpose. While money from my policy could buy my kids comfort for some years, none of that material security could spare them from the booby traps of life. If I wanted to make them a gift worth dying for, it would be a map of my experiences, mistakes, and what I wish I'd known before jumping in the water without seeing the bottom.

I realized that the one and only thing that kept everyone afloat through each flood had been love, peace and the desire to push forward. These emotional states had been the only thing worth pursuing, and I had now found it by understanding myself, what I fear most, and how I can help others avoid pain and suffering.

Now on the other side, I no longer feared failure, loneliness, or death. Instead, I feared dying without truly living or serving others, especially my children and those seeking something we can't explain, but we'll know once we find it.

For me, that is Love, Purpose, and Peace. Not the variety of images that these words evoke, but the emotional state of complete alignment with yourself, others, and life. I had stumbled upon this feeling many times before and devoted my life to searching for ways to experience it again.

Through trials and tribulations, I stumbled upon answers to my deepest questions, and ways to turn my fear into power, finding sustainable ways to experience the state I desired.

Against all odds, I searched within myself for the answers I couldn't find outside, and discovered that our biggest treasure hides within ourselves. The treasure to change the way we perceive the world, our behavior, and find in me what I had sought everywhere else.

In these pages, you will find more than anecdotes; you will uncover a roadmap to an unconventional path to love, purpose, and peace. A path that took decades to uncover, through a series of challenges and tests I don't wish on anyone.

I have written this book for you, dear reader, hoping you'll find answers to your questions, or at least avoid my mistakes. Perhaps you'll defeat your inner dragon faster, and find the emotional home you've been seeking.

Fortis Fortuna Adiuvat.
Nihil Timendum Est.

II.

Mirror Reflections: Recognizing the Dragon Within

"Knowing yourself is the beginning of all wisdom." - Aristotle

---

The pursuit of the perfect love relationship has always been my guiding star. However, the harder I tried to replicate what I saw in movies or read in books, the more I seemed to fail. To ease the pain, I sought answers from coaches, programs, and dating experts, hoping to find the secret to winning in love. From psychology to the advice of strip-club owners, I absorbed it all, thinking that if it worked for them, it would work for me.

Unfortunately, following their well-intentioned advice only tangled me further. While I improved my ability to get dates and attention, I spiraled downward in confusion and engaged in contradictory behavior; a dichotomy between what I knew and thought I had to do. The theories in these books made sense until I put them into practice, where they seldom translated into desirable results.

I abandoned my ideals of the perfect relationship when I prioritized financial status and egotistical pursuits. By my late twenties, I had achieved every material goal I had set for myself, from playing in a popular rock band to owning an international business. Yet, a successful relationship eluded me and only deepened my existential void.

Realizing that money and achievements only gave me a momentary rush of self-worth, regardless of magnitude, forced me to look in the only place I felt secure; myself. I needed to understand how

I sabotaged my outcomes, and what I could do to make a relationship work. After all, love seemed to follow definitive patterns, more like a puzzle than a game – a puzzle I felt I could solve.

Learning from two divorces and numerous failed relationships, I gathered golden nuggets of wisdom that formed the foundation for my journey. To uncover the root causes, I dug into my childhood to understand the beliefs that shaped my experience, and how I had acquired them. I journaled every traumatic or uncomfortable situation I remembered, and eventually a pattern emerged.

Change had been forced upon me through physical violence, fear, and religious manipulation. Having been exposed to these factors early on in life, I found ways to overcome them and opposed them at heart. But my attitude only got me singled out or rejected, all of which signaled that something was wrong with me. Not knowing any better, I began seeing myself through others' opinions, and found significance in gaining their acceptance.

My step-father by title — but Father by role — taught me the fundamentals of life with tough lessons, and without explaining the reasons behind them. Instead, he imposed his beliefs and perspectives upon me with repetition and force. The more he tried, the more I resented it, and sooner or later, I fought back.

Unable to sustain this way of life, I sought alternative ways to rebel, particularly engaging in activities they despised. I got tattoos, earrings, played in a rock band, listened to heavy metal, and competed in extreme sports. I ditched religion, stayed out drinking with friends and even went skydiving. These statements proved that I made my own decisions, and no one had a say in them.

Marrying at the age of 22, I emancipated to pursue my own life and cut the last thread of dependency. I dreamed of being independent, carrying my own weight instead of others', and living happily-ever-after. I now had a chance to fulfill my dreams and prove to others I was good enough.

My prideful self-perception carried over into my relationships. I used guilt or passive-aggressive behaviors to get my way, at least temporarily. Afraid of being wrong, I tried to steer every action into a predictable outcome and reduce our chances of failure. I deployed tactics I had unconsciously learned from my parents, movies, and those around me.

Ultimatums, "take it or leave it" scenarios and episodes of self-righteous indignation became common currency in our arguments. My rebellious attitude had become unbearable, and it led to the end of the road.

It took letting my dream life slip from my hands to look in the mirror for answers, and their arrival exposed my warped self-perception. I realized that I had been my own worst enemy, and if I disliked myself in the past, I now wanted me dead.

My self-perception had become distorted, chiseled by the opinions and actions of those I valued. Finding certainty in reprimands and punishments instead of affection, I approached the world as a hostile environment, always in a defensive state of mind. Based on my past experiences, I had developed a dislike for people in general, and felt no-one could be trusted.

For years, I rejected favors and kindness from others to avoid owing them favors or, worse, being taken advantage of. This approach seemed to reduce disappointment, but it also created emotional distance that led to separations and pain. Clearly, my rule had become a shackle, and it was time to break free from it.

Until now, I had been working for love, doing things in exchange of being tolerated. As a child, I had learned that the only way to avoid a put-down was to jump when asked to. And it seemed that even as an adult, I continued to follow this pattern in jobs and relationships. I crawled out of my skin to be the everything to everyone, betrayed myself to please or follow others, only to wallow in despair when I met my inevitable fate.

To manage my predicament, I gathered courage and turned against myself. What if I caused the situations I feared most? What if, anxious to know "what's next", I forced situations into specific outcomes? The glimmer of curiosity led me down the rabbit hole of self-development, and it started with the only constant in my life; me.

What if, instead of beating myself for failing, I found and addressed the underlying reasons for my behaviors and emotions? I had stumbled upon some variation of the phrase your outer life mirrors your inner emotional state many time, and perhaps questions were the answers I needed.

Without a better lead, I decided to flesh myself out psychologically and become aware of the invisible patterns the led to disastrous results.

I started by changing my inner dialogue from tyrant to supportive. Carrying guilt and beating myself for past endeavors only affected my present life, and those in it. The voice of treason tormented me with my shortcomings and inadequacies; the voice of reason whispered to go on. Realizing my unconscious actions led to dreaded results, I jumped headfirst into becoming my best friend and understanding who I am.

For the first time, I consciously discerned the voice of ego and experienced self-acceptance. Like in the cartoons of my childhood, I recognized the voices of "right" and "wrong" over my shoulders, and with them the clues to advance on my journey.

Becoming my best friend meant helping myself level-up, gaining the skills I needed to get closer to the emotional state I sought. Through introspection and self-development, I not only gained valuable knowledge about the issues that plagued me, but also shed the habits and blind spots that held me hostage. Upgrading my life experience became a simple game of "one step a day", one step further away from emotional hell, and one step closer to love, purpose, and peace.

While I initially stumbled my way upon knowledgeable mentors and resources, finding ways to unfold myself proved to be a challenging task. The abundance of material and different takes on similar topics confused more than helped me, and it wasn't until I found one of the resources below that I experienced a significant breakthrough.

It's worth to note that these aren't hard parameters of your personality. Instead, the combination of knowledge found in these, and other tools helped me create a personal "user's manual", a guide that allowed me to connect situations to beliefs, beliefs to thoughts, thoughts to emotions, emotions to actions, and actions to results.

If I knew then what I know now, I'd begin my self-discovery journey using and experiencing the following tools:

- Jordan B. Peterson's Self-Authoring Program
- MBTI Myers Briggs Type Indicator
- Enneagram Test
- IQ assessment
- Tony Robbins' UPW (Unleash the Power Within)

These tools, in no particular order, helped me form a more complete image of myself, and identify areas of improvement in my modus operandi.

Jordan B. Peterson's Self-Authoring Program

I first discovered the Self-authoring Suite in 2017, diving the internet for coves of knowledge. The program entails a complete dive into you past, present and future. Though it took me over a year to complete all assignments – mostly due to lame excuses – the self-authoring suite shed light in many aspects of my past hidden in the dark of my subconscious, but that held valuable information to re-building my life.

By undertaking the self-authoring program, I uncovered traumatic situations responsible for many of my actions. This process allowed me to address them one by one, compose a well-rounded picture of my personality, and craft a roadmap to move forward in life.

MBTI Myers Briggs Type Indicator

The MBTI Myers-Briggs Type Indicator provided me with insights into my personalities and their quirks. By exploring four pairs of preferences – extraversion/introversion, sensing/intuition, thinking/feeling, and judging/perceiving – the MBTI helped me understand how I perceived the world, made decisions and what standard features are part of my truest self.

Unraveling my personality type unleashed many surprises, both pleasant and painful. It shed light on my strengths and unique abilities, many of which I perceived as negative or hindering based on others' opinions.

The dots of my past connected in ways I didn't foresee, and the causes of my failures, and victories, became evident in my eyes. Armed with newfound self-awareness, I proceeded with confidence, making changes that complemented the best parts of me.

Enneagram Test

The Enneagram Test served as my next step into the intricacies of my personality. This powerful psychological framework identifies nine interconnected personality types, offering a multidimensional roadmap to my deeper motivations, fears, and desires. The Enneagram offered an introspective lens through which I began to comprehend why I acted in certain ways, particularly under stress.

It unveiled patterns I was previously blind to, deep-seated triggers that made me behave contrary to my conscious desires. This newfound awareness of my emotional landscape proved to be transformative. It allowed me to become more self-compassionate, patient, and open to change. By understanding my Enneagram type, I leveraged my natural strengths and worked on my weaknesses with a clear plan, catapulting personal growth and sweetening my relationships.

IQ Assessment

Embarking on an IQ Assessment became a significant part of my journey, challenging me to question my intellectual capacities and offering me insights into how I process information. It served as a bridge between my self-perception and measurable aspects of my ability for abstract thinking and introspection.

While the IQ test didn't define me or my potential, it illuminated the nuances of my cognitive strengths and weaknesses. I was no longer stuck in a binary classification of smart or not, but instead, could understand the unique dimensions of my intelligence.

This realization was humbling and invigorating. It helped me foster a deeper appreciation for diversity of thought and an acceptance of my capabilities. By knowing where I naturally excelled, and areas where I could further improve, I was better equipped to navigate my personal and professional life. It allowed me to channel my efforts more effectively, understanding that each person's intelligence is a spectrum rather than a fixed point.

Tony Robbins' UPW (Unleash the Power Within)

Tony Robbins' Unleash The Power Within event bridged the gap between psychological and physical performance. In 4 days, I learned more about myself, my psyche and how to catapult my journey than I had in many years. UPW is the event that tied all lose ends for me, connecting the dots between my psyche, my body, and my mind.

Throughout the four days, I participated in practical exercises, challenges and even a fire walk. I re-discovered a lost part of myself and new ways to experience joy and fulfillment, steering me closer to the peace and clarity I sought.

These tools provided a foundation for my journey of self-discovery, each one contributing a piece to the puzzle that is my ever-changing, complex self. Coupled with resilience and determination, they paved the path towards self-awareness, understanding, and ultimately, a personal roadmap to the feeling I longed for.

Becoming aware of my reactive side helped me understand the reasons behind my actions and uncover blind spots that drove my experiences. They offered guidance and personality-specific strategies to upgrade myself and fine-tune my approach, saving me from much trial and error. By spotting the success clues hidden within past failures, I gained a deeper understanding of what I truly desired, and how to get there.

Understanding my personality in the context of relationships allowed me to make high quality decisions, instead of guessing or resorting to instinct in demanding situations. By identifying the ingredients of my personality, I learned to appreciate unique qualities in others, while resolving "inevitable" issues became the key to fulfilling and loving relationship.

Although challenging, the first step on my journey to heal had turned out a success. Delving into the depths of my personality illuminated an unseen path, guiding me through the darkest tunnel. Now, whenever I face an undesirable situation or result in life, I look within for answers first, and find peace in knowing that real change starts from within.

III.

Battles Within: Unearthing Past Trauma

"Until you make the unconscious conscious, it will direct your life and you will call it fate." - Carl Jung

---

As a child, I only heard praise from my dad if I fought other kids or performed daring stunts. Smacking sleeping bus passengers, deflating a neighbor's tire and other mischievous behavior usually led to a nice, champ! or wow, tiger! validation I much cherished and enabled me to behave worse.

However, the same behavior my dad enabled and encouraged, was the one he punished me for the most. I carried my knack for mischief in school and around the neighborhood, and soon, I became the kid everyone avoided. As a teenager, I rebelled even more, but I learned to keep myself under control to avoid punishments or humiliation. By the time I turned 19 I had lived in over a dozen places, and being an outcast began to weigh on me.

As I got older and faced more rejection, I became resentful at those who criticized me and set out to prove that I could survive on my own. My inner discomfort grew throughout the years, and I had reached a point where anything set me off. I confronted co-workers, bosses and even my loved ones with anger, and justified my defensiveness by the pain I had been caused.

This path led me to some self-proclaimed victories, but my approach only blinded me from reality. While I thought to be winning and earning respect, those around me dispersed without noise. Eventually, I found myself alone and with nowhere else to turn. Until then, I had prided myself on not needing anything from anyone – but, as they say, pride goes before the fall.

Being proud of my self-reliance turned out to be a shortcoming. I had become incapable of asking for help, which simultaneously pushed away those I cared about. Awkward dates, failed job interviews, and offending relatives were just a few of the results of my blind behavior. Painfully, I realized my limiting beliefs contributed to the very outcomes I feared the most. To uncover these insufficiencies within myself, I resorted to therapy, practical psychology and some of the resources mentioned in the previous chapter.

Working through old traumas resembled hand-fishing for diamonds in a teeming port-a-potty. To uncover forgotten moments that had scarred my unconscious, I needed to delve into situations I had suppressed due to their content. Opening the can of memories exposed traumatic events where I had adopted a limiting belief or defense mechanism to cope with it, and future iterations.

I now uncovered the reasons behind past rejections or failures and understood my part in them. Though tempted to abandon this difficult process of introspection, the pain of past situations and admitting failure paled in comparison with the implications of failing again. I reached a turning point when, after months of searching, I discovered the root cause of my unavoidable need to reject favors and keep everyone at arm's length.

As a child, I had finished playing with my neighbors, and their mother gifted me 50 cents for ice cream, along with her two boys. It had been two months since we moved away from my grandparents' home to a small rural development. Maria and her two kids, Manuel, and Marcos, were my only friends as I adjusted to the new neighborhood. Inside our home, my father watched soccer while my mother and two brothers were out running errands.

Even though we hadn't moved far, my grandparents had been my rock for the first 8 years of my life. They taught me valuable lessons, treated me with love and affection, and shielded me from my father's punishments. But my safety net had disappeared. Just days ago, my dad punished for bringing home a Batman bottle neck hanger from the supermarket, accusing me of stealing it.

When Maria joyfully handed me the money, I took a step back as if facing a snake. Something inside me begged to run away, even though I perceived good intentions in her gesture. Unable to refuse the money, I reluctantly thanked her before going back inside.

The 15 yard walk home felt long and heavy, burdened by the uncertain future. Going back inside meant facing my dad and the unpredictable demands he placed on me. Sometimes I had to wash the dishes or gather firewood for the oven; other times, he punished me for unknown offenses, though he claimed I knew what I had done. Living with his unpredictable and volatile personality had been a challenge, and now I had to brace myself for whatever came next.

As I opened the door, an air of tension loomed before me. To avoid being accused or punished for lying, I shared the news of the money immediately. He looked at me, took the money, and calmly ordered me to my bedroom, where I was to stand facing the wall. I could hear the clinking of his metal-studded leather belt as he made his way to the bedroom. No plead served my case, and I comforted my physical pain with the fire of anger.

While reliving this event caused some inner turmoil, it also exposed the root cause for many painful situations in my life. I dodged unnecessary punishments by rejecting favors during childhood but had caused myself more pain by offending others for self-preservation. The ramifications of this perspective were wide-ranging and destructive. However, now that I recognized it, I had the opportunity — and obligation — to change it.

This event illustrates the first time I stumbled upon unhealed childhood trauma, and how it translated to adult life. Throughout my life, I have trained myself to be tougher physically, mentally, and emotionally, to become the person that can handle whatever comes next. But no amount of training or toughening up helped me feel better inside or release suppressed emotional discomfort. Recognizing and healing traumatic events allowed me to forgive and forget, so I could shed the invisible shield that kept me from my desired emotional state.

My journey took me through fears, stumbles, and heart-rending moments of truth. But in the end, it brought me growth and freedom from suffering. I had to confront my flaws, understand their roots, and learn to allow others into my life. Like that old fear, I traced my defensive behavior back to its beginnings and resolved to change the damaging cycles they threw me in.

Digging deep into my past, I realized how even the smallest traumatic moments had shaped me. The fears I had forgotten still lurked in my mind, secretly guiding my every step. They controlled my adult life in ways I hadn't even known, but not anymore. No amount of old trauma is worth the cost of a fulfilling and loving relationship.

The weight of old traumas, though heavy, would no longer dictate my present actions or hinder my future potential. Reacting poorly to past wounds only perpetuated a cycle of pain, restricting the possibilities of positive outcomes. By refusing to let past scars dictate my responses, I uncovered a pathway to transformation, allowing me to pave a road towards healing, growth, and the realization of my dreams.

IV.

Training Grounds: Preparing for the Dragon Hunt

"Man cannot discover new oceans unless he has the courage to lose sight of the shore." - André Gide

---

In Argentina, soccer holds more importance than more important things. My father played professional soccer, and that meant I was "blessed" with the gift since, in those days, jobs and vocations were often passed down through generations. To honor this tradition, he force-fed me soccer and discouraged me from pursuing my "natural" interests. His standards were incredibly high, both physically and mentally.

His love for the sport blinded him, and although well-intentioned, his burning desire to transfer his passion to me proved futile. From team mascot at 4 to punishing training regimes well into my late teens, I learned to endure them with feigned interest, yet grew resentful in my heart. The harder he tried, the worse my disposition and dislike for the sport became, intensified by the psychological torture to meet these standards. I simply couldn't develop an affinity for the sport, its culture, or even playing it; I had two left feet.

Running, calisthenics, and many other sports were also out of the question for me. My lungs weren't fully developed, and I often required injections that saved me from fatal asthma assaults. My lack of physical prowess became an integral part of my identity, and I went through elementary and high school as the kid sitting on the sidelines. I attempted to participate in class runs and soccer matches, but I was more of a hindrance than a help, often ending up humiliated by the class bullies.

By my late teens, I had embraced an insufficiency complex, believing that I lacked attractiveness, uniqueness, or even basic skills, influenced by how others reacted to me. I spent many years feeling unworthy of love, attention, or even a decent life. I had no home, money, or self-confidence, leading me to question who would ever love someone like me.

These beliefs and traits translated into my approach to love and romance, acting out my insecurities and ultimately experiencing the outcomes I feared. My lack of confidence, self-acceptance, and dating experience inculcated a deep fear of rejection, reinforcing the notion that everyone saw right through my imperfections.

My first few dates were disastrous; being my authentic self-labeled me as needy, nerdy, or slow. While hearing these things about myself made me self-aware, they also gave me clear directions on what to do next. I resorted to do more of what someone asked, and less of what I enjoyed, which seemed to yield quicker results. It appeared much easier to put on a facade than to be honest, and people-pleasing became a central aspect of my personality; my way of grasping onto others' affections.

When I finally got a girlfriend, I became obsessed and did things for love that I didn't know I could. I showered her with gifts, cards, lengthy phone calls, and daily visits, even if it meant riding the bus for 5 hours. Love songs suddenly made sense, and I found a state of fulfillment and bliss that transformed me into someone unrecognizable. Yet, this utopia was short lived, as her interest for someone else pulled us onto separate paths.

Amid the blissful façade, being dumped shocked me to the core. For the first time, I had come face to face with the dragon that lurked in my innermost fears; not being good enough. What had I done wrong? Why did this happen, and why did it hurt so much? I had gone to great lengths to how much she meant to me, yet my best attempt had only resulted in heartbreak.

Resentment consumed me, and self-hate grew, intensifying my self-dissatisfaction. To ease some pain and begin to grasp love's complexities, I turned to books and sought guidance from experts, hoping to make sense of the emotional hell I found myself in.

I devoured every piece of knowledge I could get my hands on, applying all advice to real-life scenarios as quickly as possible. Driven by my perceived catastrophe in matters of love, I gulped anything that I thought could turn my life around. Within a short time, dating became an obsession, and I set out to find that elusive emotional state once again.

As I gained self-confidence, unknown parts of myself emerged, bringing forth the joy that comes from progress and personal growth. However, amidst this progress, I felt increasingly lonely and confused. Despite socializing with people often, I still felt no closer to a romantic connection or falling in love.

Regardless of the quantity or quality of my flings, I felt as lonely as I did when I first began, perplexed when "proven" techniques failed to yield long-term results. Silent abandonment from potential partners inflicted even deeper emotional wounds, driving me to question my reasons for it all.

My dating journey took me through two marriages and divorces, as well as countless other relationship attempts. Years of trial and error had left me empty handed and without desire to go on. Something within myself, however, yearned for more.

Unraveling the solution to each problem required stripping layers of automated responses to certain triggers, hence giving me an opportunity to change the outcome. It had been a 20-year failure-ridden journey from my first breakup to my second divorce, and while I had no desire to get back up, something in me pushed me to keep going. I accepted the call and jumped back in the realm of introspection.

Connecting the dots between my worst experiences and their underlying causes—my own perceptions—filled me with guilt, pain, and hopelessness. Each confident misstep had been a charade, fooling only myself in the process. I had lost everything near and dear to me due to ignorance, and scenes replayed in my mind like a movie on repeat, searching for insight. My unaware-of behavior became painfully evident. I had turned into my own worst tyrant, tormented by the pain I had caused to myself and others.

These situations seemed insignificant at face value, but convincing myself to move on became a greater challenge than I had anticipated. Labeled with a myriad of undesirable traits, I bullied myself to become the opposite of what others accused me of, but given my circumstances, how could I be certain? Who could convince themselves they had done the right thing when reality seemed to prove otherwise?

Accepting this darker side of myself proved to be an unpleasant and humbling experience. I confronted the person responsible for all this pain—a failure staring back at me in the mirror, a reflection I encountered multiple times daily. I faced my own worst enemy, the one who had tirelessly ensured I received exactly what I feared. It was in that moment that I experienced hate for the first time, as I looked into the eyes of the man responsible for losing my family, job, and desire to live.

However unbearable my self-hate became, my two young children depended on me. Though I broke down often and beat myself to a pulp, I did it in secret and silent. I couldn't afford to let my kids see me in such deplorable state, and months of this behavior only pushed me deeper into the abyss.

Aware of the pain I could inflict on myself and others, I became terrified of making unaware-of mistakes that could lead to hurting the ones I loved most, and who depend entirely upon me. This dark part of me, who reacted faster than I could think, had ruled my life and misguided important decisions. The pain I lived in simply a result of my choices.

I didn't want to lead myself into another bear trap, and more importantly, I didn't want to drag my kids down with me. It was no longer about how my feelings or the unfairness of my circumstances; my mission was to become the person my children needed, and that required a non-negotiable process of self-refinement. I had to find negative beliefs, patterns, and traits within myself and transform them into their opposite.

Determined to become the best father and romantic partner I could be, I wasted no time in turning things around in my life. What could I do to make my partner and kids feel loved? What were my deepest yearnings and fears? Uncovering the answers became an obsession, leading me to delve into my psyche, and hunting down the dragons behind my internal struggles and failures.

Traits that I had once been proud of revealed themselves as weaknesses, consistently manifesting behaviors that I despised in others. Stripping away the mask of my hypocritical, egotistical self, stirred an internal shift—a transformative process where self-improvement became a source of joy and fulfillment. Learning to embrace the discomfort of reorienting myself became a pleasurable task, and purging myself of fears that wreaked havoc changed my life in unimaginable ways.

The first shift came from understanding that everyone, regardless of outward appearances, experiences pain and suffering in equal measure. Recognizing the importance of sparing others pain became my top priority, a firm step in the right direction.

By understanding, through experience, that all humans are fighting a silent battle, experiencing emotional and mental pain in similar fashion, allowed me to change my approach and improve my relationships. Although somewhat apprehensive with such simple approach, the changes in my life helped me understand the far-reaching consequences of my unconscious behaviors and beliefs.

With the diligent pursuit of self-refinement, I uncovered a stream of peace and repose. Addressing destructive patterns of responses spared me from repeating previous mistakes, reshaped my perspectives with a touch of philanthropy, and allowed me to experience the state of joy and fulfillment I sought.

For most of my life, I perceived myself as someone who needed to survive in the world, constantly protecting myself from unknown, but guaranteed, dangers. However, this new perspective opened my eyes to the beauty of life that I neglected by favoring being right, instead of feeling right.

The rewards for learning how to focus on the areas that truly matter have been incalculable, filling my life with magical moments, joy, and fulfillment. Unlike goals and accomplishments, understanding that we are perfect works in progress removed the burden of comparison and self-imposed pressure, translating into emotional states that I had sought after my entire life. By realizing fears are simply answered questions, self-development became the tool to solve my innermost riddles.

I understood, through experience, that success is a feeling, the feeling derived from the pursuit of a meaningful goal. And what could be more meaningful that working on the source of all your needs, desires, and dreams; yourself?

V.

Stoking the Flames: Slaying Relationship Atrophy

"Love does not consist in gazing at each other, but in looking outward together in the same direction." - Antoine de Saint-Exupéry

A stagnant relationship always frightened me, stirring endless debates about the merits of long-term commitment. The concept of exclusivity, however, appealed to me the most; a pact between two people abiding by the unseen principles of a "relationship." Yet, the thought of failing to maintain a romantic bond after a certain stage seemed inescapable. In previous attempts at long-term success, familiarity crept in, and without notice, our dynamic changed from passionate lovers to tolerant roommates.

I repeated this pattern multiple times, until I became aware of its existence. By taking each other for granted, we drifted apart as the initial jolt of joy faded, finding more faults in each other. After certain point, situations seemed irreconcilable, and they brought out the worst of us.

The failure of stumbling upon this issue in every relationship – whether with new items, jobs, or partners – forced me to search for a sustainable way to keep passion alive. Was every relationship destined to fail? While I didn't care much for going through another tour of pain, the alternative was living with the regret of not trying my best. Knowing I couldn't live with my conscience if I ignored this call, I dove on a search that eventually consumed me.

In the past, I scrutinized every situation and considered possible alternatives to predict the next step, and ways to wrestle with it. But this process taxed my mental health and often produced erroneous predictions. I became frustrated with trying to decipher the code for a successful relationship and became fearful of never finding a solution. Above all, I sought to prevent further emotional damage for myself and my partner. If I could avoid potential pitfalls, I could perhaps embrace love rather than battling to preserve it.

However, problems surfaced when one or both of us could no longer hold back our frustrations. Unvoiced transgressions built up, bred resentment, and led to unexpected, destructive eruptions. We seemed to strive to ruin each other, using words and tactics designed to cause maximum pain. Our intimacy became a weapon, and our words reminders of why we don't show vulnerability. Recognizing this pattern exposed a crucial key, but escaping it appeared nearly impossible. Reaching this point usually resulted in separation, as neither acknowledge our faults, or cared to make up for them.

Unbeknownst to me, the hidden fear of abandonment drove me to try harder, usually choosing to endure the storm and see things through. Bur most partners didn't reconsider their decision, and the few who did didn't stay for long, forcing me to evaluate my behavior and the steps I could have taken to avoid such miserable results. While blaming ex-partners evoked short-lived relief, my perfect record of failed relationships proved I had work to do.

Scared of repeating these destructive patterns, but too exhausted to continue fumbling forward, I sought a method to understand my partner's needs and my role in them. Fear of experiencing unjustified abandonment compelled me to pursue the truth, even if it meant facing painful realities. During this quest, I found many strategies to keep a relationship "alive," all burning bright and fast, rather than serving as a solid foundation for long-term sustainability. Romantic gestures like gifts, activities, and trips were great for boosting morale quickly, but often led me to ignore underlying resentments.

To solve my predicament, I began asking my partner for direction or preferences on topics I considered fragile. I involved her in all my decisions to avoid unforeseen problems. If something could threaten the security of our relationship, I wanted to handle it long before it showed up. My new approach, however, suffocated my partners mental space, and it took a few relationship flops to get the point.

Nonetheless, my new behavior produced valuable insight, realizing that I did save myself lots of headaches by asking questions, and I just needed to adjust my approach. The missing piece of my puzzle appeared during a podcast episode of The Tim Ferriss Show, where I learned about the "1 to 10" method.

Instead of typical vague questions like "What's wrong?" or "Are you okay?" to acknowledge mutual tension, I began asking my partner, "On a scale of 1 to 10, how good of a partner have I been this week?". This new way of asking enabled my partner to share her honest challenges, and find ways to improve. No matter the score, I would then ask, "What could I have done differently to make it a 10?" I listened carefully to her feedback and suggestions, revealing crucial aspects that might otherwise remain hidden.

Applying this new habit required time and practice, but the rewards were instant and significant. By inviting constructive criticism, I gave my partner a voice to express her fears and challenges within the relationship. Our bond strengthened as we both openly and receptively engaged in this process, ironing out the wrinkles of our bond. By requesting my partner's feedback, no matter its content, I stumbled upon an opportunity for mutual growth and fulfillment rather than a chance to take jabs at our weak spots.

Old triggers and misconceptions sometimes influenced our dynamic, evoking familiar emotional responses from our past. However, I recognized this as part of the healing process, avoiding becoming defensive or offended by taking things personally. While no approach is perfect, submitting to the scrutiny of constructive criticism paved the way for the rewarding relationship we both desired. Like every other aspect of life, if we're not progressing, we're regressing, and neglecting certain aspects of our lives will inevitably lead to their decay and eventual end.

Yet, surrendering your ego to just 10 minutes of 'mental martial arts' a week can do more than revive fading hope — it can ignite a spark, fueling passion and determination. The intrinsic value, intimacy, and fulfillment drawn from these sacred moments are undeniable, and can only be experienced to be appreciated.

These weekly heart-to-heart encounters have become a space for us to mend rifts, patch up holes, and lay bricks towards constructing our dream love fortress. All this transformative journey required was the tweaking of a few words, the eagerness to genuinely listen, and the courage to confront the dragons of my inadequacies for the sake of slaying them and nurturing growth.

This invaluable approach helped craft a map, detailing land mines, traps and areas of improvement before stepping into them. It exposed traits my partner valued, and I ignored, and I found peace knowing which direction to take.

Open to a challenge? During the next week, try implementing the '1 to 10' method in your relationship. Ask your partner to rate you and be prepared to listen to their answer without defense. How did it make you feel? More importantly, what changes did it inspire?

VI.

Taming Reactive Dragons: The Invisible Power of Silence

"Meditation can reintroduce you to the part that's been missing." - Russell Simmons

***

Much has been written about meditation and its benefits, so I'll focus on its impact on my relationships and self-understanding.

Meditation has held my fascination as a field of personal experimentation since I first experienced Yoga Nidra at age 13, during a high-school theater class. I rediscovered meditation at 20, and it has served as a miraculous tool, bringing about changes where other obsessive efforts fell short. From my athletic days to my current roles as a father, partner, and entrepreneur, meditation is a non-negotiable part of my life.

Initially, however, meditation puzzled me. The discomfort of sitting still ranged from pain in my lower back to the chatter of my restless mind. Worries, impending tasks, potential problems - all haunted me. The longer I kept my eyes closed, the bigger they seemed to become. After a few sessions – 4 – I abandoned shadow boxing and sought other ways to satisfy my curiosity.

Hypnotherapy emerged as an attractive tool for improving my motocross racing performance. Despite skepticism and a fear of ridicule, my ambition for success overshadowed my doubts. I eagerly purchased a selection of audio courses, drawing early guidance from Jack Canfield, Tony Robbins, and Dr. Jay Granat.

Visualization, slow-motion replaying, and inner work to enhance outer performance seemed obscure until I experienced the results. My performance improved rapidly just by thinking about it - a life changing revelation. However, an injury curtailed my sports career after three years, and I left both competition and mental exercises behind.

As time passed, I noticed my mood souring and my reactions becoming more impulsive. Trivial issues irritated me, and minor problems haunted me for days. Uncomfortable in my own skin, I took up mountain biking, Krav Maga and exercising to release my negative emotions.

While my activities alleviated stress and restored some emotional balance, moments of rash decisions still influenced my life. I considered myself even-tempered yet caught myself making promises when elated and important decisions when angry. This behavior had now cost me jobs and relationships, and slowly deteriorated my emotional state. To deal with this issue, I resorted back to meditation and resolved to making it a part of my life.

Before I could make this permanent change, I had to understand how meditation worked, the many types and styles, and how they translated into my life experience. I toiled with guided meditations, hypnosis, ASMR, Transcendental Meditation, Yoga Nidra, visualization, and other more obscure techniques. Books, neuroscience, and psychology podcasts helped on the intellectual side, removing the stigma of my misconceptions. After understanding how each practice fit into my life, I found a sustainable way to justify my new habit.

Within a few weeks of daily practice, meditation increased the gap between a stimulus and my response, uncovering ingrained behaviors that I ignored. As my mind became less reactive, previously alarming situations no longer sparked a fight/flight/freeze response, allowing me to make higher quality decisions. The merits of this non-reactive state extended beyond my personal life; I rid myself from prescription drugs, reduced the burden of exercise, and set myself free from the guilt I experienced after reacting and hurting someone else.

Furthermore, meditation boosted inner rest, creativity, and clarity while diminishing stress and other harmful influences. The reactive side of me that jumped when triggered seemed happier and relaxed. This more balanced mental state helped me curb emotional eating, impulsive purchases, and defensive behaviors - all contributing to better mental, spiritual, physical health, and ultimately, emotional utopia.

Meditation may not resonate with everyone, but its potential advantages merit exploration. As I discovered, there is often a gap between preconceptions about something and its true value, which becomes evident only through direct experience. Providing the mind a well-deserved break from its incessant grind can produce surprising results, irrespective of age or background.

In the past, I disregarded meditation due to societal pressures and my ignorant perception of it, based on others' opinions. My shortsighted approach deprived me of a valuable life tool and a reservoir of ancient wisdom. When I finally mustered the courage to delve into it and commit to its practice, I unearthed a treasure far beyond my expectations - a treasure that transformed my life and the life of those around me.

My journey with meditation is a testament to its power, reminding me that the dragons we fear often guard what we value most. Once tamed, these beasts can guide us toward a life of tranquility, purpose, and fulfillment. After all, there is 'no grail without dragons', and every journey starts with the decision to explore beyond the known territories. You can only free your mind by taking small steps at a time and realizing there's nothing to fear.

I now believe that the greatest adventures often lie in the unexplored depths of our own minds. In there I found the answers and keys to the life and relationship I dreamed of. And just like me, meditation could be the key to unlock that immovable object. Who knows? Your own dragon might be waiting to be tamed, and to become a driving force at your every command.

VII.

Double Dragon: Facing an Unconscious Beast

"Until you make the unconscious conscious, it will direct your life and you will call it fate." - Carl Jung

My journey to self-awareness started with an unsettling realization: I unknowingly behaved like a dictator. Throughout the years, I masked my defensive actions by believing to be the one "saving the relationship" and looked to my partners for apologies and resolution. As a father, I rationalized screaming or breaking down in tears as a by-product of emotional exhaustion, and circumstances that pulled me underwater.

Frustration brewed within me, and to my detriment, others around me validated my behavior as acceptable. While I felt some relief from the emotional beatdowns I subjected myself to, the acceptance of those around me kept me blind from the destructive power of my actions, not once hinting that something had to change.

A nagging conscience, however, told me I was straying off-course. The guilt and self-loathing I felt after every episode overwhelmed me, grasping for solutions to my inner torment. Despite my attempts to ignore or ease this inner discomfort, I seemed chained to this path of destruction.

While I spent weeks exploring hypnosis, journaling exercises and other tools for self-improvement, it was a confrontation at a local park that shook me awake. My children, caught in a typical playground squabble, faced an irate father's threats. On spotting this, my inner composure crumbled, replaced with the urge of making this grown

44

man feel what he'd done to my kids.

Before I could reach him, my children sprinted towards me and clung onto my legs, an act that snapped me back to reality, while the man walked away. Although I initially savored this perceived victory, introspection soon replaced my satisfaction with self-reproach.

A wave of awareness washed over me. Could I have handled it better? Could I have been less confrontational, more diplomatic? If I believed no one had the right to intimidate children and I had done a good thing, why didn't it feel that way?

The bitter truth hit me. I saw in that man what I had done to others, and if anyone deserved my wrath, it was me. Throughout my life, I displayed the same behavior with my children and romantic partners, instilling in them the same negative feelings I despised. For the first time in my life, I witnessed from the outside how I had made others feel.

If no one had pointed out my negative behavior, it was because they feared me and wanted to run away. In my heart, I believed that behind my actions were good intentions, but my delivery achieved the opposite. By removing the blindfold, I could now see where I strayed off the path.

I set to find the reasons for my behavior and ways to manage it. Through self-discovery exercises, I unearthed the root of this dark side and gained clarity. My past was fraught with punishment - physical, psychological, and emotional - for failing to meet others' expectations and standards. This had translated into an unchecked anger that surfaced during stressful situations, unexpected events, and even trivial issues. I had become a living dichotomy; the victim turned victimizer.

Revisiting these moments, I recognized my tendency to shield myself against feeling inept, at the cost of others' well-being. The more

I dug in, the clearer my cowardice became and with it, my desperation to change it. Having bullied those I loved by lacking temperance stung more than I expected. Under the guise of "preventive damage control," I had behaved in ways that evoked guilt and self-loathing, imitating those I resented.

My behavior didn't just hurt others. Acting this way with partners and friends left me feeling guilty, frustrated, and eventually, alone. In the past, I wallowed in the need for answers and direction; what had I done wrong? Now, I had gotten what I wanted, and realizing others had left me because of my intolerable behavior crushed my soul.

Determined to turn things around, I adopted a 'people over things' philosophy and pledged to guard my family from further hurt, beginning with myself. My family's total sense of well-being dwarfed any job, challenge, or achievement that had previously consumed me. My kids and loved ones didn't ask to be around me, and if I wanted to keep their precious company, I had to change my approach.

This revelation humbled me. I lived not for myself but for them; my children who had no say in their father's choices, and my partner, who stayed despite infinite alternatives. I once read "God's gifts to us are our friends and talents; our gift to God is what we do with them". My family depended on my best version to thrive, and the best thing I could give them was what I longed for all along: selfless support, love, and affection. With the sword of why in hand, I set off to slay this troublesome snake.

My search led me to dive into old memories, fears and situations that had marked me in a way related to the events that triggered me. I knew that my intent had always been good, yet I expressed them with anger, intimidation, and borderline frustration. I didn't want to see my kids or partner walk into a trap, but by forcing them to take a different path for their own good, I reacted in ways I repented.

This sense of entitlement, and feigned authority, had only led to a deplorable emotional state. Despite my best intentions, I had avoided possible issues at the cost of definite pain. I had reaped what I sowed. In that moment, I understood that reciprocity ruled; only by embodying love, respect, and affection could I receive them in return.

This fresh perspective brought about an unexpected emotional shift. The more I focused on giving with a genuine intention, the more fulfilled I felt. Most of my pursuits weren't for material gains, but to achieve an elusive emotional state, and my approach seemed to be getting me closer to it.

A few months later, I crossed paths with the same man at the same park, while our kids played together. He seemed to recognize me and started walking in the opposite direction. I called out to him and waved; he stopped and waited – reluctant – by his car. I extended my hand and introduced myself anew. I apologized for my past behavior and expressed my gratitude towards him.

His reaction that day helped illuminate a blind spot in me, a flaw that had caused much damage in my life and the lives of others. I felt a sense of humility as he listened silently, his eyes softening as he accepted my apology with a simple nod. His small act of forgiveness confirmed the changes I'd made, underscoring the power of transmuting my negative patterns.

As I returned to my kids, a sense of relief washed over me. I had conquered my blind spot, made amends, and stumbled upon peace and respite. By facing unaware-of behavior, I eradicated the patterns that resulted in pain, guilt, and self-loathing. My past was a mixed bag of mistakes and regrets, but now, I had a new perspective to understand my actions and a chance to become the person my family deserved.

Managing and overcoming my destructive patterns, I embarked

on a path paved with compassion, empathy, and love — a path I considered for the weak, but took the most strength to walk. Because it's not the lessons we impose in others that matter, but the ones we teach through our actions. We're not just the beasts we perceive in the mirror; we can also become the hero we aspire to be, and the safe haven our loved ones need.

VIII.

The Dragon's Hoard: Tearing the Mask of Greed

"To ease another's heartache is to forget one's own." - Abraham Lincoln

━━━◆◆◆━━━

What does it take for a person to become selfless in a world that often rewards selfishness? I grappled with this lesson from a series of harsh realities and from losing those I loved due to misguided values. At 17, I found myself living alone in a dangerous city to finish high school. Soon after, I migrated to the U.S. equipped with nothing but a carry-on.

Years later, I roamed worldwide, soul-searching after a painful divorce. Each of these different environments shaped my personality and perspective of the world. While I quickly learned how to adapt to new places, survival often required a 'me first' approach.

My early years in the workforce thrust me into a defensive mode of living, propelled by an unspoken race for wealth and status. The environments I navigated emphasized one thing: safeguard your achievements, because others won't.

I first encountered this philosophy as a six-year-old, enduring punishment for breaking a vase. Later in life, an employee recommendation gone wrong cost me my job, and have weathered multiple breakups for damaging valuables.

These events underscored the significance of accumulating more than others and protecting it fiercely. I internalized this lesson, reinforced by those who punished me for damaging their belongings. When the time came to have my own, I reflected this behavior onto others.

For many years, this approach served me well, sparing me countless uncomfortable situations. I developed an aversion to accepting favors, not wanting to be later reminded of them or feel indebted. I strived to stand on my own two feet, keen to evade the condescension of others' charity. However, my approach didn't seem to work in love and dating, but I wouldn't find out until years later.

In my early 20s, I fell in love. I proposed to my partner after less than two years of dating, and we married young. I showered the early days of our marriage with affection and romance, doing everything in my power to keep our passion alive. However, as a novice in long-term relationships, I misunderstood their true mechanics. I focused on making her happy, unconsciously seeking validation in return, all in a bid to maintain our blissful state forever.

My mind began turning when I felt that the feeling wasn't mutual. A subtle shift in our dynamic distanced us, and I began to gauge her responses to quiet my insecurities. At the same time, I talked myself out of the relationship by comparing my expectations with reality, and her current behavior with her initial enthusiasm.

I yearned for the exhilaration and deep connection of our early days; a connection that seemed elusive as we passed the one-year mark. In my desperation to salvage our relationship, I turned to nagging and comparisons, which, unfortunately, only exacerbated the issues.

In less than a year, I morphed into a controlling, insecure, and paranoid individual. If something seemed amiss, I interrogated her with suspicion, using an accusatory tone. As if I laid traps for myself, I became spiteful and hurtful when I got the answers I elicited.

The emotional canyon between us broadened as we focused on

separate activities and people instead of spending time together. We found ourselves drawn to others, defending ultimatums with self-righteous indignation. To ease some of our tension and mutual resentment, we took time apart from each other, spending it with friends and family.

On Memorial Day, with beaches ready to open in New Jersey, my partner and I planned to meet up. She had stayed at a friend's place after a concert, and we agreed to meet at our favorite spot for breakfast. I called her early and throughout the 3-hour drive to meet up, but my calls went straight to voicemail.

At first, I considered it a technical issue. But after spending the day without news of her, worry consumed me, and I raced home. When she finally called back, I grilled her about what happened and expressed my disappointment. She apologized, seemingly unconcerned, and ended the call after my tirade.

I packed bags in the living room for our next day trip when she walked in. She bypassed me and headed straight to the couch, sinking in it arms crossed. Then, with firm words, she said, "I want a divorce." I stuttered in disbelief, considering it a cruel joke. While I knew we traversed difficult times, I believed we could weather the storm together. Is this a joke? I asked. But she remained stoic. When I repeated my question, she said the same words again. In that moment, reality's brick smashed my face; she meant every word.

I trembled, gasping for words or even direction. I perched on the coffee table in front of her, struggling to understand the situation. Suddenly, the life I thought I had would soon vanish.

During her time with friends, she felt loved and appreciated, something I had failed to give her. I wracked my brain for solutions, asked for forgiveness, and promised to change. But it was too late. Regardless of how much I recognized my mistakes or repented for my actions, I had had ample time to treat her right, and I didn't. Now, I faced the consequences for ignoring my intuition in decisive moments and justifying my ignorance.

My world collapsed within 24 hours. The life that took years to build vanished within seconds, and I only had myself to blame. At 24 years old, I found myself alone, without any family, and having failed at what I yearned for most. Within a few months I quit my job, surrendered my car to the bank, and soon after my sports bike got stolen. I plunged to the abyss, losing everything I had worked for.

With no clear direction or purpose, I embarked on a two-year journey across the globe. I sought something that I couldn't define - a passion, a purpose, and a soulmate to share them with. My deep need to find love and dodge the sting of abandonment pushed me towards untried avenues, including a second marriage.

This marriage, lasting seven years and blessing me with two beautiful children, ended in ways I never could have anticipated. The accumulation of years, relationships, and failures stripped me of everything except one stark realization - without love, nothing else bears significance.

Twelve years after my first divorce, and with my current partner, I found myself in a similar emotional situation. Unemployment, the COVID-19 quarantine, and living in a small apartment with my two kids and golden retriever beat me to a pulp. My then-girlfriend and I lived in different cities, about 30 minutes apart. After two years, her lease ended and instead renting an apartment together, she moved in with us. My apartment was small, but the chance at living together excited — and scared — me.

Having lived in worse places, I didn't see an issue with us cramming into a one-bedroom apartment. We didn't plan to stay there long, just enough to settle some debt and move out together. But after a few months, I got laid off and became unemployed.

The first few weeks of unemployment brimmed with opportunity; time to spend with the kids, travel and look for another job. I had some cash saved, money in the bank and plenty of prospects for work. Six months later, I found myself desperate for work, digging into my savings and racking up debt.

The situation at home grew tense, and I began making trivial comparisons. The disappointment of getting what I wanted, regardless of all these things I did for her, urged me to confront the situation. I pondered how someone could feel comfortable in another's home without contributing. She had a job, money and knew I was unemployed, yet seemed unconcerned with financial responsibilities.

I wrestled with contempt for weeks, until the inner pressure forced me to face the issue. Within the last few days, I had built a fool-proof case to state my point and elicit a change in her behavior. But when the moment arrived to address the situation, something inexplicable happened. I found myself unable to deploy my well-crafted plan.

Despite having valid, logical, and constructive arguments, time seemed to have stopped, giving me the chance to reconsider my approach. It was then that I recognized the ring of intuition again, and this time I obeyed it. Following the voice of ego might give me a feigned sense of importance or validation, but I knew where that led, and I chose to try the opposite.

Instead of treating my relationship like the stock market, I became thankful for being able to support her and my children through a time of change. Living with a divorced father of two could not be easy, so why would I make it more difficult? If I was able to make her life easier in any sense, including easing the burden of financial pressures, then I would do it wholeheartedly. This approach seemed dangerous and vulnerable, but also the path to a deeper level of connection and joy.

She appeared less stressed, happier, and involved in activities she enjoyed. She traveled, visited family, and had the opportunity to explore life, knowing I supported her unconditionally. I recognized the value of self-exploration and the importance of encouraging her growth. Contrasting what I expected from relationships with the joy of giving selflessly made my choice clear. I continued to give and support her, regardless of any initial discomfort. The phrase people over things became my guiding principle.

While this approach seemed counter-intuitive, the heightened sense of fulfillment and inner peace I derived from it marked my direction. The more I focused on giving and doing for others, the better my own life seemed to get. Even without money, cars, or material possessions to share, I found joy in being of service and improving the quality of life for my loved ones. For the first time in my life, I discovered the source of joy I had been seeking, and it hid under the boulder of selflessness.

Switching from a what's in it for me? mentality to what more can I give? change my life and helped me shed the belief that things are meant to be defended. It is others' that are to be protected, and things to be enjoyed with them. At the same time, knowing that I have given my best effort pulverized all fears of abandonment. By defying the perspective imposed by others, I acquired my own, and with it the power to experience love, purpose, and peace.

My journey to selflessness has taken me on a winding path, marked by intense trials and deep introspection. Through personal experiences, I have learned to prioritize the happiness of others over my own expectations or desires. I've understood that true love does not seek to control or demand. Instead, it nurtures and encourages growth, joy, and selflessness.

This shift in perspective has imbued my life with a sense of sustainable fulfillment. By pouring into others selflessly, I discovered the emotional satisfaction that had eluded me. Concentrating on what I could offer others, rather than what I stood to gain, endowed me with a sense of accomplishment and completeness I hadn't found anywhere else. And in a surprising turn of events, I found the emotional state I had dreamt of, all while relishing the pleasure derived from aiding others to flourish.

Transitioning from a self-centered perspective to one of selflessness, I unearthed hidden joys veiled beneath the burdens of ego. This journey, illuminated by trials, tribulations, and profound introspection, led me to conquer the dragon of greed, tearing through its veil of illusion. My new perspective revealed the essence of selflessness, promising authentic happiness that transcended material possessions. And the treasure I found echoed the dragon's hoard, a treasure not in material riches, but in heart's transformation.

IX.

Guiding Flames: Lighting the Path with Invisible Principles

"To see what is right and not do it is the want of courage." – Confucius

<hr />

By living in over 35 places around the world, I've come to understand that every society has its own set of rules and consequences for acceptable behavior. Whether it's fines or the loss of personal freedom, there's no shortage of red tape dictating what we should and shouldn't do.

Much like children, I'd been forced to accept certain rules or be punished for ignoring them. I had received fines for speeding, gotten fired for missing work quotas, or berated for not bringing in enough money. When it came to breaking rules set by man, the consequences seemed to be only financial and temporary. While I experienced a state of anxiety and uncertainty prior to being judged, I shed the fear of consequences once my hard-earned dollars left the bank.

However, when it came to relationships and marriage, there were no established institutions ensuring that couples upheld their vows or treated each other with decency. Whether I decided to lie, cheat or be the best partner ever, there were no evident rewards or punishments. The invisible principles of a relationship were agreed upon by the soon-to-be partners; a mutual agreement signed in trust and hope. But no-one except us could abide by them, something that became difficult once the real intentions behind our actions emerged.

Getting into a long-term relationship based on lust, insecurities or fear only led to destruction. Like signing a bad loan out of desperation,

I made promises to others without fully comprehending the implications. This lack of understanding and wishful thinking led to many dead ends, losing people I loved and experiencing humiliation due to self-imposed denial. I longed for someone who would love me unconditionally and not leave, yet I often ended relationships due to inexplicable reasons.

After a few months of dating, I started comparing the amount of effort invested versus the perceived benefits. My desire to stay together waned, created conflict, and eventually led to our breakup. Even though I recognized this pattern, I kept repeating my mistakes by ignoring my inner issues, and instead looking for excitement elsewhere.

Flirting with coworkers, texting strangers, and engaging on social media became coping mechanisms for me, providing a temporary ego boost. I justified these actions by convincing myself that if my partner didn't know, no harm was done. It allowed me to momentarily feel better about myself and approach my relationship without the fear of rejection; someone else thought I was enough. However, the feelings of guilt, paranoia, and fear persisted, even though I managed to escape the consequences of my behavior. Although I avoided getting caught, I felt increasingly worthless, somehow knowing I headed for disaster.

This pattern of testing the truth began in my youth, and it continued under my radar until my second divorce. It was then that I understood those unseen principles were real, unknowingly proven through my own actions. I had tested my luck, overlooked the wisdom of the ages as just old wives' tales, and the backlash of my ignorance knocked me off my horse.

My life experience served as proof - alone, without a home, and recently out of work. I associated these outcomes to the things I had done behind my partners' back, actions that caused turmoil and consumed me from within. From my missteps, I understood a hard truth: every action inevitably ignited an equal or opposite reaction, whether they played out mentally, physically, or emotionally. This wasn't just a concept from my high school science class; it applied to every facet of my life.

Stripped of everything, I refused to build anything new in life. For four long years, I had bunked on strangers' couches, hiked miles to work, and struggled to maintain a life overseas, all to bring my family with me and shape a future together. Now, I was out of that picture.

The realization that I could have acted differently to avoid this pain sparked a desire for change, pushing me to shift my perspective rapidly. If I had any doubts about the aftermath of lies, lust, and taking my partners for granted, I had no choice but to let my experiences speak for themselves. Any lingering doubts about the value of principles and rules in a relationship were banished by the weight of my own experience.

In Argentina, I learned the phrase, "When eyes don't see, hearts don't feel", an all-too-common justification for lying or stealing. I had internalized this belief to justify my wrongdoings and avoid the consequences but understood – through massive failure – that moral principles exist for our protection, not as a means of oppression. To agree and follow a mutual agreement with my partner, even when not in their presence, meant to avoid pain and suffering by knowing what to expect next.

The first step in adopting this new perspective was to understand what truly mattered to me. Did I want to keep trying my luck and proving myself a fool, or find the love, purpose, and peace that I sought? If my own approach and rebellious behavior had resulted in the opposite, perhaps I needed to search where I least wanted to look.

Why did I oppose authority? Why did I consider moral principles pointless? A thorough introspection revealed decades old trauma with abusive authority and religious institutions. I recognized my unconscious response to hypocritical teachings, principles taught by the very same people who broke them. I had witnessed those around me commit – and punish me for – the sins they preached against, pushing me on a journey to find my own answers, what worked, and what didn't.

Experienced proved to me, beyond reasonable doubt, that it was in my best interest to consider the experiences of those before me. Each time I deviated from what I considered right for the relationship, I paid in emotional pain and suffering, the very same state I worked tirelessly to escape.

The key to escaping old misconceptions dwelt in challenging myself to do what's morally and ethically right, regardless of the potential outcomes or personal inconvenience. I've abandoned the fear of being hurt because I've already hurt myself to an unbearable degree. I've chosen to be open, vulnerable, and honest, recognizing the importance of integrity and adherence to timeless principles for my own well-being.

The phrase "I DO" now holds a new world of meaning for me, whether as a verbal agreement or marital vows. It represents two people promising to push forward together, understanding that the emotional state experienced in a solid relationship obliterates that of money, status, or achievements. I had been through them all and refuse to walk that path again.

That's not to say I don't wrestle between reasoned choice and impulsive behavior. I have faced situations where the self-serving route seemed easiest, avoiding the worse of two poisons. But having taken that path before, I could only consider one approach; the uphill battle to reprogram myself and embrace moral soundness. Surprisingly, gaining this new perspective became easier than I thought. Choosing what felt right in my heart freed me from guilt over doing what I knew was wrong.

Like any habit, retaining my responses required conscious effort at first, much like learning to play the guitar. To learn basic notes and chords, I forced my fingers into odd shapes and calloused their tips against the strings, struggling to make a palatable sound. With proper repetition and practice, I eventually learned to make music and enjoy the creative process. You can only experience the music of moral soundness by trying it out yourself and fearing it's consequences over others' opinions.

My career, money, the pandemic, divorce, unemployment, and illness have all presented "easy way out" options, tempting me to act solely in my own self-interest. But the pain embedded within me reminded me of where those seemingly inconspicuous decisions lead. It emphasized the importance of love above all else, especially the temporary relief of my short-term, but suffocating, anxieties.

The ropes of a mutual agreement and moral principles now serve to keep us on the path we both want to follow. We understand what's acceptable in our relationship, learned to respect our desires and non-negotiables. Doing what's right and trusting that things will work out has become my guiding light in every endeavor, eventually leading me to the end of the dark cave where the love, purpose, and peace I sought had been patiently waiting.

X.

Lost in the Smoke: Patience as a Healing Force

"Have patience with all things, but chiefly have patience with yourself." –
St. Francis de Sales

Throughout my life, I have learned that the meaning of patience is wide and varied. In my childhood, I expressed repressed anger through pranks and troublemaking. Being told don't do X pulled me headfirst into doing it, even in relationships. I often heard phrases like, "You're lucky I'm so patient," or "I don't know what else to do with you". While I did my best to avoid a scolding, getting in trouble seemed wired in my DNA.

My high school years followed a similar pattern, with teachers patting themselves on the back for tolerating me. I found myself in the principal's office three to four times a week, and my parents were often called in for disciplinary issues. At one point, I faced expulsion for standing up to two bullies during recess. It felt like I balanced on a tightrope. If I allowed others to bully me, my dad would reprimand me at home. But defending myself also got me in trouble, and I grew confused and without direction.

I adopted this approach in relationships and jobs until I realized there was no correlation between my level of submissiveness and favorable outcomes. I accumulated resentment by agreeing to things I disliked, and later beat myself up for losing.

Tired of feeling let down, I adopted a rigid mindset: it was my way or the highway. I clung to patterns that made me feel safe, demanding those around me to meet my strict expectations. When they failed, my patience evaporated, replaced by anger and harsh words. I felt justified, believing I had endured enough, but I didn't realize I was burning bridges between me and those I cared about.

While being a difficult child had challenges, adults and their expectations were more complex. I repeatedly heard how difficult I was to deal with, which increased my frustration. Neither being patient nor oppressive had produced positive results. If I repressed my reactions, I felt resentful. If I let them out, I experience guilt and self-loathing.

I wrestled with the practical definition of patience for some time, until is essence became clear to me. After my second divorce, I got laid off and cared full time for my two toddlers. Learning the ropes of single parenting proved challenging, and patience became fundamental on my path.

For the first time, I saw myself through my parents' eyes. Whether pleading with my kids to go to bed or take a bite of their meal, my tolerance between expectations and reality got tested daily. Within a few months, I learned to suppress my negative emotions, but the toll often surfaced in silent breakdowns.

One day, I crouched on the floor next to the bed after a panic attack. I battled the voice of inner criticism and guilt to find purpose and direction. Max and Bella enjoyed a snack in the other room, while I disappeared to unload my stress. Before heading into the bedroom, I asked them to play after snack to avoid spilling food or milk on the floor. It had been the same situation twice that day that sent me hiding for a break.

Now on the floor, I questioned myself and the reasons for enduring such tribulations. My breaks consisted of breaking down, beating myself psychologically, and looking for answers to the pain. I snapped out of my self-imposed cage at the sound of their laughter, followed by liquid splashing on the floor. The scene revealed their food and drinks over the recently cleaned floor, their clothes, the wall, and even the dog. A feeling of powerlessness washed over me, and I started screaming in disbelief.

The rant lasted a few seconds, until I noticed the fear in the eyes of my kids. I knew deep in my heart that no situation justified such behavior, yet here I was, having reacted out of instinct. My inadequacies as a man, father, and romantic partner had led me to that point, and it was my job to get out of that hole.

Through research, I discovered the profound impact of a child's early years and the boundless potential that could be stunted by misguided expectations. This realization forced me to question my demands and confront my false sense of superiority.

My personal failures, including two divorces, numerous job losses, and frequent panic attacks, were glaring evidence that I still had much to learn, especially patience. I knew that I couldn't allow myself to behave that way again, and to achieve that, I had to understand why I snapped in the first place.

Some digging into trauma archives exposed my issue. When situations didn't go my way (the way I considered best), I feared negative outcomes on my loved ones and expressed my desperation through impatience. Wanting to avoid painful outcomes drove me to act irrationally and become blind to the behaviors that caused the issues in the first place. It dawned on me, then, that I didn't need to be patient with others; I had to be patient with myself while I shed and managed unreasonable expectations.

This new perspective made logical and emotional sense to me. I began questioning myself at the first sign of frustration, creating space to spot my misconceptions, shortcomings, and a better way to react. Thus far I had been the cause of my own problems, but could also become the solution and the one to enjoy the results.

From that afternoon on, I turned a new page and shed the skin of impatience and erroneous perspectives. Gradually, my peace of mind began to increase, and I retrained myself to react in constructive ways. This approach served me well when I entered my current relationship, and I became aware of how my new views translated to love and romance.

By allowing others to grow, and pushing past my comfort threshold, I learned to detach from outcomes and trust the process. My relationships, especially with my partner, blossomed in unexpected ways. My children became more confident in their abilities to make mistakes and get back up; my partner found relief when I helped her instead of giving her improvement tips. My life was no longer a battlefield, but a shared journey of growth and understanding.

Freed from anger and resentment, I embraced forgiveness and self-compassion. What I once misunderstood as patience became my most powerful ally. True strength comes from understanding, nurturing, and accepting others.

In learning to be patient with myself, I learned to love better, live fuller, and embrace the beautifully imperfect journey that is life. The path has not been easy, but I would walk it again and again. The meaning of patience now shines clearly, lighting the way to a future filled with hope, love, and understanding.

XI.

The Inner Struggle: Unraveling the Serpent of Commitment

"Commitment is what transforms a promise into reality." - Abraham Lincoln

---

For many years, my romantic life followed a familiar and unchanging cycle of infatuation, abandonment, and heartbreak. While school taught me certain subjects and family shaped my manners and principles, no one prepared me for the winding and turbulent road of love.

The burning desire to find "the one" drove me to seek love in many places, learning valuable lessons along the way. Despite my willingness to fail forward and get back up, many years of failed relationships had taken a toll on me, especially after two divorces. Ever felt like life is stuck on repeat? That's how I felt for years.

To find my soulmate, I explored relationships with women from varied backgrounds, nationalities, and social strata. Whether a fleeting connection or committing to marriage, each relationship seemed destined to end with one heartbroken and the other eager to depart.

But I wasn't alone in my predicament. Many couples I knew seemed happy at face value but confessed their relationships had dwindled for years, and were headed for divorce. I had experienced this firsthand in my parents' relationship, multiple romantic connections, and two marriages. The common issue? They weren't ready.

After my second divorce at 36, I questioned whether all relationships were destined to wither and perish. In both instances – and many casual relationships – the issue seemed to be the same: one of us wasn't ready to commit. While this excuse belonged in dating, it did not have a place in marriage. How can one enter such a serious commitment and not be ready to honor it?

I had no rational explanations, and while I preferred to be single for the rest of my life, I couldn't ignore the burden of failure. What does "being ready" even mean? To find the answer, I had to understand what I wanted to be ready for. After two divorces and a consistent breakup record, I blamed myself for not knowing what to do and carried enormous guilt because of it. I had to find a solution, and fast.

The first stop in my journey was a hard look at my own actions. I often convinced myself that every partner was 'the one,' clinging to that ideal even when evidence suggested otherwise. My unrealistic expectations led to disappointment and resentment.

The pattern became clear. When I first met someone, I exaggerated traits I liked in them, and ignored the red flags. I endowed them with all kinds of positive traits and behaviors, even if we hadn't known each other for long. Most partners seemed to do the same with me, and I became addicted to the short-lived rush of falling in love.

But failing to sustain that emotional state, I strived to find that feeling in new connections. By recognizing how my needs muted the voice of intuition, I uncovered the first deadly error in my approach. To deal with this issue, I resolved to prioritize reasoned choices and my intuition, versus making decisions based on fear or need.

Integrating this new approach into my life took some effort, but it helped me overcome the fear of exercising my power of choice. I had gotten myself into lots of trouble by making rash decisions, driven by the fear of missing out on love. By recognizing the first domino in the line – idealizing others – I could now stop myself from repeating the same mistakes.

Life tested my resolve by introducing many women between my second divorce and my current relationship. Some held powerful jobs, others wanted to hug trees and save the world. In the past, I would have compared this potential partner to ones that didn't meet my expectations and gotten entangled in the same old predicament. This time, however, I understood that I demanded from others what I needed to change in myself; ultimate commitment. This small perspective shift propelled me in the right direction and one step closer to my goal.

The second clue appeared while digging into my past. I analyzed fights and arguments from previous relationships, fishing for clues to my puzzle. Among the plenty of fish I caught, one stood out.

One summer afternoon, my mom invited my first wife and me for dinner. That night, my brother, my wife, and I sat at the round table, picking on each other and having fun. Once we got bored with telling jokes, we switched to talking about cars and bikes. My brother and I had recently purchased a new sports bike, and it became the center of our chats.

During our talk, I confessed to my brother about ordering some performance parts for the bike, and my excitement to try them on. While he approved in excitement, my wife expressed her concern for my safety and desire to get rid of such a dangerous toy. "I'll get rid of you before the bike," I said to her, in a sarcastic tone. Although we laughed it off that night, it took me years to realize that my joke had played a key role in my demise and exposed a dangerous blind spot.

Besides my hurtful sense of humor, that memory connected to many others where I had prioritized my hobbies and fun over the person I wanted to be with. The times I missed my chance to make things right became evident, along with the results of my poor choices. I recognized my selfish behavior and the many instances others had warned me about it. It took losing it all to value what I had, a common thread in our human experience.

I understood, through trial and error, that a good relationship is the foundation for overall success in life. Each time I prioritized work, friends, or hobbies over my partner, I put a hole in our love boat. My blind behavior drilled holes rather fast, and I then blamed others for jumping out of a sinking boat.

Becoming aware of my unconscious actions shook my world; this other side of me had led me to pain and failure, despite my good intentions. This reactive part of me took control when I felt threatened or scared, and acted in ways I wouldn't have otherwise. If I wanted a long-term relationship, I had to become the type of person others wanted to be around. This meant retraining myself to act, and react, in ways that aligned with commitment and the goals I pursued.

Convinced of my new approach, I followed my intuition and tried, for the first time, to genuinely put others' interests before mine. New situations, people, and circumstances presented multiple opportunities to benefit at others' expense. But no matter the challenge, I kept my approach and stumbled upon a newfound sense of inner peace. Commitment became a rope in the dark, a guide during times I couldn't see clearly.

Although my approach got tested by fire — exes reappearing from the ashes, getting an ultimatum from my partner, and even an eviction notice — I handled each situation with a refreshed perspective and objective. Having eyes for my partner only, and understanding the reasons why this benefited both, gave me a newfound sense of confidence and purpose. I thought I had it all figured out until the last piece of the equation came into play during a rough patch in our relationship.

At that time, my partner and I faced challenges due to exigent circumstances. She moved into my one-bedroom apartment, where my two kids, dog, and I lived. Her grandmother fell sick and forced her to travel often, while the emotional aftermath of my divorce still stirred issues between us. The chaos made it difficult to distinguish between "us" and "me," leading to many fights and tentative breakups. Also, the pressure of living in a cramped space had become unbearable, forcing me to weigh my options for the sake of both me and my children.

To find a solution, I resorted to emotionally distancing myself from her, and often pointed out her behavior towards me. I conveyed my concerns and explained we couldn't continue this way. While this situation would warrant a breakup in other circumstances, I preferred to find a solution for everyone's benefit, instead of tasting the pain of failure again. My experience proved that I caused the situations I feared most, hence changing partners was not the solution.

However, my partner didn't think the same, and acted out her emotions. She complained often, became distant, and let out all her frustrations during our arguments. Her behavior instilled in me the need to fight and flee, but instead, I tried a new approach.

To spare ourselves the pain of regret—and intuitively knowing it wasn't the end—I suggested she visit her family for a break. The tension at home worsened, while my partner hadn't seen her family for months. The COVID-19 quarantine allowed her to work remotely, and my lease would expire in 10 weeks, presenting a perfect opportunity to heal and reassess ourselves.

Although this suggestion sparked insecurities within me (what if she meets an old spark and I'm gone?), I felt confident in my approach. I knew in my heart that two willing partners could work through anything, and for me, encouraging her to take time off during our worst moments represented a genuine gesture of love, trust, and commitment.

My partner agreed to take the trip, and she landed in Arizona two days later. She planned to spend two weeks there, coming back home a few weeks before moving. Once the two weeks had passed, she decided to extend her trip, although not knowing for how long. I approved and encouraged her to do so, but the alarms of breakup rang loud in my head.

I have always believed that people vote with their feet. In the past, many partners professed their love for me only to leave me for someone else; jobs praised my performance only to fire me without cause. In the case of my partner, her decision seemed to point to an end between us, and I had to wrestle with — and accept — this fact.

While on her trip, I stumbled upon an old female acquaintance at the local bookstore. We had met during my mall working years, and had formed a friendship by hanging out with her and her sister after work. Neither of us had shown romantic interest in the past, and I considered her to be the only female friend I had had.

Among our many updates, she announced that she worked nearby and moved into town. She explained that she had moved there to finish college about a year ago, and had another year before going back home. She seemed eager to chat and called or texted me a few times a day. I welcomed the company and conversation; after all, I hadn't been in contact with many people since becoming a single dad, getting laid off, and going into quarantine.

Our previous friendship encouraged me to vent, and I allowed myself to share personal fears, looking for insight into my relationship issues. As a woman, perhaps she could share wisdom from a different perspective. I confessed to going through turbulence with my current partner and shared the latest events in search of a pattern. As our chats grew longer, the feeling of familiarity set in and doubts began to surface. Had I committed to the wrong person?

To make matters worse, her attempts to comfort me further confused me. I had been my only emotional support thus far, learning to rewire my inner dialogue for respite, instead of judgement. But receiving encouragement and support from someone else resembled putting on a sweater on a cold day; I didn't know how much I needed it until I felt it.

The swarm of doubts and fears overwhelmed me, and I set out to understand my situation. I knew in my heart that I did not want to be with anyone else, that all could be worked out between two willing partners, and where jumping ships led. It wasn't a matter of disbelief or superstition, but one of experience and intuition. While my mind spewed logical reasons to consider alternatives, my intuition led me through the smoke.

On what turned out to be our last chat, she confessed her crush on me, and bombarded me with reasons to be together. But before that, my partner and I had argued over the phone for no apparent reason, and I couldn't help but vent my frustration. As I explained my conundrum, she seemed to understand and say the right things. I contemplated my options and envisioned the possible outcomes, but only out of fear and confusion, not desire.

My ego screamed for validation and certainty, my Soul for honesty and integrity. Also, I began to realize that my fears were imaginary; I tensed up, suffered from anxiety, and looked for alternative options when I felt scared and confused. But this time around I resolved to understand my situation, and within an instant the answer became clear.

Avoiding that situation felt like keeping two magnets apart, but I knew from experience where that path led. In the past, I had allowed primal instincts and ignorance to blind my choices, paying for my actions with failure, pain, and regret. This time around, however, I caught myself, and stepped firm in my commitment towards my partner.

I thanked her encouraging and flattering messages and told her we could no longer talk. I explained that although I faced relationship turbulence, escaping my fears would hurt my partner, children, myself, and her. Peace of mind and relationship integrity meant more than the impulse of connection, and I wanted to prove it by respecting her, my partner, my kids, and myself.

Days later, the last piece of my puzzle emerged from reviewing that conversation. While I questioned myself for rejecting the advances of someone who seemed genuinely interested in me, I felt an immense sense of relief after my choice. The overwhelming sense of alignment and peace underscored my assertive choices and the direction to follow.

To be ready for commitment mean putting myself aside — including my fears — and finding ways to overcome my insecurities. It also meant we had work to do, and if we both wanted to thrive together, we had to chip in the same amount of effort. By blindly committing to each other we made our choices clear, and simple; if it didn't contribute to our well-being and love union, we did our best to avoid it, or manage it.

By changing my inner dialogue and perspective, I acquired the confidence to know what it feels like to be ready for commitment. The realization that no other adventure in life is as fulfilling, thrilling, and sustainable as a love relationship helped steer my choices in the right direction. My old self-serving approach and fear of missing out led me to justify ignorant choices that hurt others, including myself. But being ready to commit meant understanding challenges, issues and temptation will arise; the foundation of trust that keeps everyone afloat.

My journey allowed me to release the burden of past mistakes and take control of my happiness and fulfillment. The cycle of infatuation, abandonment, and heartbreak that once imprisoned me finally vanished. I discovered that being ready for a committed relationship meant having the courage to love fully and unreservedly, while keeping the snakes of doubt out of my head. To love someone is a choice, and I learned to prioritize it above all else. By becoming ready for long-term commitment, I threw away all the outside distractions that kept me from growth, fulfillment, and love, allowing them to flow into my life.

XII.

Hidden Treasures: The Fire Within, A Torch in Darkness

"Life is really simple, but we insist on making it complicated." – Confucius

In my younger years, I was a prisoner of desire, held captive by the allure of physical attraction. My pursuit of admiring women and seeking their acceptance was an unquenchable thirst, rooted not in love but in a need to prove myself. This obsession with appearance had its roots in childhood when my father, with high physical expectations, forged my mentality through forced exercise and hindering remarks.

From the age of 5, my father force-fed me his passion for soccer and expected me to follow in his footsteps. Given that I seemed to be cut from a different cloth, he resorted to extreme physical workouts and explosive teaching methods. I could be a champ or tiger if I performed to his expectations, or a cocky fat kid when I didn't.

Throughout elementary and high school, I often sat out activities due to asthma or other excuses, preventing me from bonding with classmates and isolating myself out of fear of rejection. I didn't want anyone else making fun of my athletic incompetence.

Feeling like an outsider among my peers, dating attractive women in my 20s became a desperate attempt to alleviate my inner torment and prove my self-worth. I had worked to get fit, lease a sports car, and rent my own place, and in my achievements, I found the confidence to approach anybody I found attractive.

To my surprise, I did better than expected and got to date anyone

I wanted. However, I soon realized that physical beauty had no correlation with relationship fulfillment or how I felt towards someone. While their physical beauty lured me out of the cave of insecurities to face the dragon of rejection and ask for their hand, the thrill of my conquest wore off once we realized we weren't right for each other.

In the best-case scenario, a romantic partner and I had agreed to split up and have a good life. In the worst, I had endured a second divorce, became homeless, and unemployed. Whatever led me to these excruciating endings needed to be addressed before I messed up again. The only consistent pattern became the excruciating pain of breakups, directly proportional to my lofty expectations and emotional investments.

After my second divorce, a haunting pattern emerged; the same cycle of failed relationships had repeated itself over a span of 19 years. From my first girlfriend at 17 to a second divorce at 36, the only constants had been my expectations, failures, and myself. I could blame every partner for their wrongdoings in the past, but I realized that I made low-quality choices driven by something beyond my understanding. This drive had been responsible for my many romantic endeavors around the world and for the traps I ensnared myself in.

Realizing that a fundamental change was essential, I embarked on a quest to understand my romantic choices' underlying reasons. I started by seeing a therapist, who gave me the first clue by asking: "Why do you think you chose your partners?" Her question sparked my curiosity, and I embarked on finding out the real why behind my choices.

After about a year of shuffling through content and learning about relationships, I stumbled upon a Tony Robbins podcast where Mr. Robbins discusses the six core human needs, and what they entail. By working around the globe helping people of all backgrounds, Mr. Robbins and his team identified the six needs that drive our behaviors: Certainty, Variety, Significance, Connection, Growth, and Contribution.

After the podcast, I delved deeper into how these needs manifested in my daily life, and how they translated to my choices and results. In that moment, I recognized my core driving need to be Significance, and the pieces clicked. I understood that I pursued a feeling, not an outcome, and connected the dots between my choices and my failures. The rejection of my early years, coupled with childhood trauma, drove me to work to be loved or accepted. I had forcefully given my all to feel significant or needed, to people who didn't want to be around me.

This discovery wasn't merely a breakthrough; it was an awakening. It provided me with a clear framework to address the pivotal factors that had governed my life, opening doors to profound understanding and personal growth.

I realized that my investment in relationships mirrored my need to feel important, a need I satisfied by placing others on an unattainable pedestal. But blinded by the resentment of their rejection, I focused on others' perceived ingratitude, never pausing to consider my role in nurturing the very pain I sought to escape. This realization both liberated and humbled me. I had unwittingly become the person I not only disliked but had worked tirelessly to avoid—a needy individual driven by fear of abandonment. Accepting this truth, and more importantly, transcending it, required courage and vulnerability.

As the need for significance continued to be my core driver, my perspective underwent a profound transformation. I realized I found significance by doing things for others, not by getting anything in return. The lack of retribution served as bait for my ego to stir the nest, but by then I had long gotten my payout; the feeling of having made someone's life better. This mindset shift not only enriched my personal relationships but also provided universal insights into human connection.

I realized that in the dance of life, there are countless ways to meet our needs and those of our loved ones, without falling into the traps of guilt and pain. Discovering my innermost need allowed me to become a better partner and build a roadmap to joy and fulfillment. My new beliefs opened the gates onto an uncharted path, one that led to genuine connection and self-realization.

In understanding what drove me, and how to get it, I discovered the timeless wisdom of empathy, balance, and the authentic power of vulnerability. It's hard to believe that such an inconspicuous perspective could have such an impact, but I have proven it to myself.

I had journeyed through relationships, marriages, jobs, and businesses looking for a taste of that feeling, only to come back home empty-handed. But once I identified what I needed, I realized it had been available all along. The opportunities to experience what I yearned for most without the tribulations of poor choices are within our reach at every moment.

Now, as I walk along a path guided by self-understanding and empathy, I can't help but wonder: What drives you? What core need shapes your decisions, relationships, and life? Uncovering this truth could be the key to unlocking a life of authenticity, connection, and fulfillment. Isn't it time for you to find out?

XIII.

Embers of Trust: Burning the Veil of Lies

"To thine own self be true." - William Shakespeare

Growing up in Argentina, I became acquainted with lies, theft, and betrayal ever since I can remember. The addicts next door, fake ads on the newspaper and even those close to me lied and concealed the truth to achieve their goals.

At the age of six, I was first exposed to deceit when I witnessed a neighbor exit our garage after stealing something, only to later deny it. From that moment on, lies became evident throughout life and an inevitable part of the recipe. While I felt strange catching my parents, neighbors and pretty much everyone else hiding the truth, it also meant I could do the same.

Lying became a tool that allowed me to sail through life without immediate repercussions. My everyday life entailed school, caring for my brothers, and waiting for my dad to give me chores. However, I led a double life where I nurtured secret interests, such as collecting Spawn comics and Metallica tapes, rebelling against my father's teachings by concealing the truth.

In the past, my dad had made promises to help me deal with my personal issues, only to punish me when I confessed what they were. His broken promise signaled that nothing was sacred, and the punishment one I'll never forget. From that moment on, I lied and hid the truth to avoid pain.

I kept my façade well into my late teens and had expanded my testing grounds to jobs and relationships. During interviews, I feigned my interest for the job to secure an income; among friends, I exaggerated the magnitude of my accomplishments and relished in feigned admiration.

With each small lie, the deceit grew, until I realized I only lied to myself. Despite knowing that lies were universally disliked, I justified my approach based on having done the right thing in the past, and losing. Lying became a means of self-protection and acceptance. It spared me from punishment as a child, shielded me from rejection in relationships, and even helped me get jobs for which I wasn't qualified.

While lying protected me from immediate consequences, – a scolding, a breakup or getting passed for a job – it gradually consumed my emotional well-being. Every time I lied, a subtle feeling of misalignment or weakness washed over me. Others might have believed what I said, but I didn't, and held myself accountable indefinitely. The high of others applauding my act evanesced when I compared reality with the imagined version of me.

Despite these feelings, I continued down a path of self-deception, convincing myself that my lies didn't hurt anyone. I considered myself better than others by the car I drove, how much I made or the clothes I wore. When I couldn't afford luxury items anymore, I bought replicas and lied about that. I exaggerated my earnings, experiences, and private life.

Over time, lying became a skill I mastered, driven to manage my low self-esteem and get an advantage in life. It's not that I mastered lying — I think everyone intuitively knew — but the inner dialogue after missing the mark. I trained my inner coach to stop beating me when I messed up and get me excited about the future.

The real dilemma lay in justifying my unethical behavior. I convinced myself that (white?) lies were harmless and that I only gave myself a chance I otherwise wouldn't get, rather than profiting at others' expense. I knew that with time, I would master whatever I lied my way into — work, sport, relationship — and would earn my rightful spot. But under all the justification, I still felt the rattle of my intuition, begging me to avoid the wrong path.

I didn't heed the voice of my conscience until the painful experience of my first divorce. I got married at 22 and emancipated from my parents to start a new life. But our relationship was full of obstacles, challenges that we had brought upon ourselves by lack of honesty and integrity. We both had lied to each other about a myriad of things, and our lack of trust eventually led to the demise of our marriage.

The seemingly perfect union I had envisioned disintegrated as lies were uncovered on both sides, eroding our mutual trust, and ultimately leading to divorce. We had both twisted the fabric of truth with good intentions, but like the invisible principle of gravity, we did not escape the price of our lies. Like a home on a sand foundation, a relationship erected on dishonesty only led to my emotional collapse.

My life spiraled downward, and I found myself alone, consumed by guilt, self-loathing, and a profound sense of disbelief. The person I planned to spend my life with went from head over heels to running for the hills. The benefits of lying had been short-lived, but the poison in my soul seemed to last forever.

After my divorce, I buried the pain of failure by dating, traveling, and engaging in extreme sports. I spent nearly two years vagabonding around the world and continued a journey of self-deception until my second divorce, when the connection between dishonesty and tragedy became undeniable.

During this marriage, I toned down the level of exaggeration, but I still lied about a few things; knowing how to dance salsa, my whereabouts, and personal purchases. Like in the past, by concealing the truth I felt weaker inside, but I rather dealt with pointless guilt than a marital fight.

No matter the size of blunder, all lies eventually emerged. She discovered my two left feet during a night out at a salsa club, a solo trip to the beach because of a parking ticket, and an expensive backpack hidden in the trunk. My actions didn't warrant lies, but the fear of upsetting her and risking another loss pushed me to do things I disliked less.

We got divorced by the 7-year mark, and from that moment on I decided to be honest with everyone, especially myself. It became clear that my issues were the result of my poor choices, and I now feared the consequences of lying and dishonesty, over the instant reactions to telling the truth. By now I had learned to fear nothing other than the consequences of my actions, and I understood how honesty goes a long way.

Lies stripped others (and myself) of the ability to make informed choices, abusing trust without considering the emotional effects on everyone. Whether white or rainbow, lies made everyone feel the same; betrayed and hurt. Furthermore, covering the original lie with more lies became exhausting and unsustainable, increasing life's difficulty.

I realized that every attempt to achieve my goals through dishonesty had been a mistake—a cowardly act driven by ego and fear. Telling the truth, on the other hand, promised to save me from the prolonged pain of living a lie, and the outcomes I feared. Even if intimidating, telling the truth meant escaping the mental prison of paranoia and guilt.

Transitioning to a life of honesty, or at least refraining from lying, exposed some dichotomies of life. I became aware of the fear that gripped me when faced with the choice to lie or tell the truth. If I lied, I might get my way for now, but I will suffer until I pay for it later, and then I'll suffer some more. But if I told the truth, I risked upsetting a partner, a boss or even myself, and would have to deal with the unknown consequences.

It had become too easy to choose the perceived notion of instant freedom over the potential long-term consequences of lying. Almost a trained reaction, I felt the urge to conceal the truth when the estimated outcome of a situation didn't align with my desires. But my reiterated experiences proved that this self-protection mechanism had caused me more failures than gains.

To try a different path, I stopped myself from speaking every time I felt the urge to lie. By recognizing this trait, I became aware of the physical sensation prior to acting it out and replaced it with silence. Instead of saying things to please others or avoid problems, I chose to take responsibility for my actions and opinions. After all, lying made me a coward and a victim to others' truths.

With growing confidence in my intuition in the face of unexpected challenges, I embarked on the next stage of my journey. Upholding an honest existence set me free from the torments of deceit, although I still felt guilty for the things I had done before. Life gave me a taste of what I had done to others, a poison that opened my eyes to the problems I caused, increasing the burden of guilt.

To ease my pain and that of other's, I sought forgiveness from family and close friends. Starting with the smallest lies, I made amends with those I hurt and worked my way up to my most shameful actions. This approach seemed to work for all involved; I freed myself from emotional dead weight, and I admitted my wrong doings to those I hurt.

Although skeptical at first, I had no other choice but to try this approach. The fear of being ridiculed, rejected or even worse, blamed, nearly stopped me from starting this vulnerable journey. However, no amount of self-deceit or justification eased the pain of guilt, and I preferred to face the consequences of my actions head on. After all, I had earned them.

To my surprise, every time I sought forgiveness form others, I not only found it, but a broken bridge was rebuilt. Most of those I hurt also regretted the trivial situation, and making mends opened my eyes to a fountain of joy and peace.

Having a clean slate, I embraced honesty and integrity as the bridge over emotional pain. Interactions and relationships with others changed for the better, and I shed the weight of old regrets. Self-respect and integrity led me to a new emotional space; a place where I felt at peace with the past, the present, and the future. The strength, confidence and trust that bloomed in my life dwarfed the perceived consequences of telling the truth, proving to myself – through experience – the adage "the truth will set you free".

Growing up in demanding environments forced me to adopt lies as a weapon and tool. They were the keys to a double life, a shield against pain, a way to fit in and get ahead. But they were also my ball-and-chain. As I grew older, the lies became my captors, locking me into a life of hollow triumphs and broken relationships.

Today, I've broken free from that prison, not by learning new tricks or mastering new skills, but by returning to something far more fundamental: the truth. The simple, unvarnished, often painful truth. It had been there, waiting for me, a path not taken until it became the only path left.

As I walk this new road, I feel the echoes of my past, the lessons learned from a tough childhood, the many broken promises, and my own double life. But rather than weighing me down, these memories empower me; they are reminders of where I've been and what I've overcome.

I'm no longer the child who accepted lies as an inevitable part of the recipe of life. I'm no longer the young man who twisted and turned reality to fit a self-made illusion. I'm someone who has embraced integrity, love, and respect, not because they are easy or convenient, but because they are and feel right.

The lies that once seemed to define me have been replaced by truths that empower me. My journey has taught me that the truth doesn't just set you free; it makes you whole. The shadows of deceit that once filled my world have given way to a life filled with light, understanding, and authentic connections.

I've come full circle, from a world where lies were the norm to a life where honesty is my guiding star. The path has been long and fraught with obstacles, but the destination has been worth every step. The little boy who once witnessed a theft and learned to lie has grown into a man who has stolen back his integrity and learned to live a life of peace. In doing so, I've not only reclaimed my soul but opened the door to a future filled with genuine joy, trust, and love.

XIV.

Charting the Path: The Compass of Clarity

"The only Zen you find on the tops of mountains is the Zen you bring up there." - Alan Watts

───────────◆◆◆◆───────────

I came to understand clarity not just as the wisdom gained from past experiences or what I didn't want in life, but as a beacon guiding me away from the dragons of low self-esteem, self-doubt, and fear that haunted me since childhood.

Rejection, not feeling good enough, and fear of ridicule turned me into a people-pleaser early on. This pattern persisted into adulthood, shaping the way I approached relationships. By fearing being alone, I often got trapped in commitments, only to later realize I had set the trap myself. To make others happy, I justified things that bothered me or signaled trouble, ignoring the possible consequences once the initial rush disappeared.

My past experiences had taught me about certain traits, patterns, and pet peeves that I needed to avoid, yet my deep longing for companionship and fear of loneliness overshadowed my true desires. Despite promising myself to be prudent and patient, my desperation resulted in destructive choices based on blind commitments. I rationalized that anything could be worked out later and jumped into relationships against my gut.

This destructive pattern had cost me jobs, friends, and marriages. It didn't matter how long must-avoid list grew; there always seemed to be new things that bothered me. Before my first marriage, I ended relationships impulsively, breaking up with partners for the most trivial of issues.

The value of clarity began to take shape after my second divorce, which shattered the family I had dreamed of building. For three years, my second wife and I worked tirelessly to overcome the mountains before us. We built our family while on separate continents, enduring the immigration process, and constantly working to reunite.

However, four years after achieving our goal, our relationship deteriorated, and soon we found ourselves accusing each other of countless offenses. Our initial after-work coffee dates turned into criticism matches, blind to the damage we caused to each other and our kids.

The situation resembled hell on earth; everything I had worked for turned out the exact opposite. Like my first marriage, dream career, and business ventures, the mirage disappeared when I reached it and instead fell into quicksand.

Over a short period of time, a pattern became evident between my actions, her reactions, and my follow-up. Until now, I had suspected the issue to be the constant nagging and mutual criticism. And while that held true to a certain degree, another equally important factor remained unseen.

I had been great at demanding what I wanted, but I was oblivious to—and dreaded—my many responsibilities. It was easy to ask for more affection, attention, or love, but the number of labels we had slapped on each other drove us further apart from our goal. Relationships are 50/50, and I knew that, but somehow forgot to treat my partner the way I wanted to be treated.

The bitter truth became evident; I had been sailing without a compass, lacking clarity about the reasons behind my behavior, and the responsibilities that came with those choices. I had been blind to the tidal waves that were automatically set in motion when I chose a certain path, and then resented my situation by blaming it on others.

In that moment, I realized why no one wanted to be with me. The need to prove my point and have my way became an evident pattern in my approach. But not once did I stop to ask or think about what my partner really needed, blind to the effects of my behavior on others.

Now aware of the actions that caused me disdain, I had to understand why I reacted in the first place. I juggled different concepts, including fear of abandonment, anger, and insecurities. But once I got to the bottom of the barrel, the issue became clear.

Like getting into a bad loan due to dire need, I justified the high, long-term interests for easing short-term anxiety, and became resentful at the time to pay. In my case, I jumped headfirst into relationships and jobs to later realize the cost, feeling trapped, and acting out my emotions. The results were no surprise.

Having clarity, then, meant understanding myself enough to know what I needed from a relationship (see Chapter 12), how much that meant to me, and becoming aware of my limits — the last being an important key in avoiding resentment and issues in the future.

Clarity did not simply become a concept or a tool, but the compass that guided me to my true north. Through self-reflection and understanding, I learned the value of not just knowing what I wanted, but also being aware of my responsibilities and the needs of others. It taught me that relationships were more complex than rigid lists or impulsive leaps into the unknown; they required empathy, attention, and the wisdom to navigate the intricacies of human connection.

No longer a reckless adventurer jumping into commitments, I became a more thoughtful traveler on the path of life, guided by the compass of clarity. I understood that even if I chose not to be in a relationship, recognizing my weaknesses, strengths, and what truly mattered could still transform me. The fog of confusion lifted, and the way ahead became bright and clear.

I didn't just conquer my fears or vanquish metaphorical dragons; I found wisdom, strength, and direction within myself. Clarity was not just a lesson learned; it embodied a challenging journey, a victory achieved, and the key to the door of new possibilities.

Whether in love or other aspects of life, I was now equipped to move forward with insight, purpose, and understanding, having a clear map of the traps to avoid. Clarity became more than a concept; it was my anchor in a chaotic world. The veil of ignorance that concealed my path had lifted, replaced by the light of fulfillment and hope. Abandoning my reckless choices and constant struggle gave way to a sustainable feeling of peace, harmony, and fulfillment.

No longer was I lost; the compass of clarity guided me with confidence and grace. In understanding myself and others, recognizing my responsibilities and embracing empathy, I found direction, purpose, and joy. My journey continues, but now I travel with a sense of ease, a soul touched by wisdom, and a heart open to endless possibilities.

XV.

The Siren's Song: Escaping the Melody of Lust

"The expense of spirit in a waste of shame
Is lust in action..." - William Shakespeare, Sonnet 129

My earliest recollections of taboo talks are filled with classmates poking fun at my indifference. They wasted their high school years giggling about this topic in corners, while I was absorbed in books or video games. This pattern had become a nightmare; friends chasing romantic liaisons at the expense of other pursuits, and my parents expressing concern over my prolonged singleness.

Although I felt like an outsider for not conforming, I found solace in Anime, TCG games, and other creative ventures. A secret longing to summon the courage to ask a girl out lingered, but the desire to avoid the limelight and dodge rejection prevailed.

The norms dictated by classmates, friends, and even some family members conflicted with mine. They urged me to pursue women when I'd rather be engrossed in any other activity. Failing to adhere would brand me a coward, the chicken scared to ask a girl out. I resisted, however, dodging occasions that might have challenged my perspective.

By 20, my belief in waiting for intimacy until marriage remained unscathed. An inexplicable affinity for this notion existed, but I kept it private to avert further humiliation. Despite a heartbreak at 18, I ventured into the dating scene, an arena filled with a myriad of personalities, experiences, and disappointments. I never struggled to attract someone I fancied, yet maintaining the connection proved elusive.

Years of fruitless relationships beat me to a pulp, a sentiment underscored by the actions and expectations of others. The pressure to conform, to transition into the next phase of life – an intimate partnership – overshadowed my preferred way of life.

Eventually, I caved in, welcoming the possibility of intimacy with another. Perhaps this missing connection contributed to my poor self-esteem?. A few months into dating someone new, I succumbed, and the moment seemingly everyone, but me, had anticipated finally unfolded.

In an instant, I satisfied the silent expectations of many and uncovered a new facet of life. A wave of relief washed over me as the need to dodge intrusive questions dissolved. Simultaneously, I grappled with a sense of confusion and disappointment. This is it?

Tormented by doubts, and regretting the dismissal of my original intentions, I embarked on a quest for clarity. Physical intimacy morphed into a fascinating exploration of the mental, spiritual, and relational aspects of my life. Dating became a quest for approval and significance, with the ultimate display of trust serving as the journey's reward. But repetition exposed a pattern. I had idealized intimacy, consistently dismissing the unease that followed each encounter.

Every intimate moment felt like another piece of me slipping away, signaling the end of another relationship. The mystery evaporated, mutual interest waned, and a predictable cycle of emotional pain and disappointment in one or both partners ensued.

Breaking up was never in my vision, but physical intimacy and the deep emotional attachment it entailed often left me disconcerted. I treasured promises, vowing only those I could uphold. Yet here I was, compromising my own values, committing to relationships that clearly lacked a future.

My freedom bore a heavy price: the pain inflicted upon others and the remorse for my thoughtless actions. Heartbreak's agony, learned through experience, prompted a years-long quest to reinvent myself and dodge future anguish. The fleeting ecstasy of climax was eclipsed by the enduring torment of guilt; one lasted a moment while the latter haunted my conscience for years.

Nevertheless, my longing for companionship led me to ignore my intuition and fall into the same old traps. I perpetuated my dating routine, facing the same pitfalls in my search for the ideal partner. Relying solely on lust, desire, and physical attraction birthed pain, disappointment, and wounds that demanded years to heal.

It became clear that I needed to change my approach and perspective. Admitting the significant role that aesthetics, lust, and physical contact played in my life was a tough pill to swallow, aware of their painful aftermath. Lust had become my Achilles' heel, guiding most of my decisions. The transient pleasure it offered was surface-level and ephemeral, yet the emotional aftermath was abysmal.

The pivotal moment in my journey dawned when I acknowledged that relationships built solely on physical attraction were unsustainable. I had proven it to myself time and again, and expecting a different outcome was foolhardy.

In relationships, seeking attention or approval from others often resulted in infidelity and heartache. In dating, it clouded my judgment and squandered valuable time on fruitless endeavors. Decisions rooted in desire became a clear red flag if I sought to preserve self-respect and my partner's well-being.

I also realized that my desire was finite, and I squandered it on superficial distractions – half-dressed celebrities, risqué dating shows, and other women. This bombardment of erotic content led me to unconsciously compare my partner to others, focusing on what I didn't have. This initially absurd theory, when put to practice, bore immediate results.

By consciously focusing on my partner and her numerous beautiful attributes, she regained her rightful place at the center of my universe, and our passion reignited. The same way I had focused — and worked for — attention and approval from others, I could replicate it with my partner. It wasn't a matter of lust or attraction; it was a matter of shortsightedness.

Much like looking down at your car after riding a new one, letting the emotion of lust point my direction had led to empty gains. It blinded me from recognizing my partners beauty and attractiveness, leading me to unconsciously withdraw attention and affection from her. This behavior contributed to our emotional distancing, and eventually the breakups I feared.

This newfound clarity about lust's destructive influence allowed me to appreciate the profound value of intimacy and vulnerability. The sense of purpose and belonging I sought was not in physical acceptance, but in mutual respect, genuine connection, and valuing my partner over anyone else.

Reflecting on my past, I now understand that my early resolve to resist the pull of lust was more than a rebellious act. It was a cry for a deeper connection, one that transcended physical boundaries, and that could grow into the emotional home we bought sought. And although it took years of painful lessons to fully grasp the essence of love and intimacy, a small perspective change revealed that the person I wanted most stood right by my side.

XVI.

Warrior's Rest: Unbinding from the Armor of Abuse

"The gem cannot be polished without friction, nor man perfected without trials." - Chinese Proverb

---

In the dark alleyways of my memories, belts, punishments, and humiliation tell tales of abuse mistaken for discipline. By 7 years old, I had grown accustomed to the sting of a leather belt when I didn't follow orders. My father believed that adversity forged stronger men and punished me like an adult.

By 13, I viewed these instruments of torment as routine lessons for any shortcomings in behavior, academics, or physical performance. He pressured me to play soccer, to fist-fight other kids around town for his amusement, and to keep the pain inside. If I didn't, I'd face the type of pain I dreaded most: emotional. Name-calling, humiliation, and exercise as punishment made me hate every second of my existence.

I endured this treatment for nearly two decades, until I rebelled and began making my own choices—often contrary to my parents' advice. Freed from my father's expectations, I felt a surge of self-confidence and relief. I no longer wrestled overnight factory jobs that tortured my soul or carried guilt for taking time for myself. I kept my earnings, and no one judged me for my preferences.

This newfound freedom helped me escape the shadow of my parents. No longer fearing their opinions or the possibility of physical harm, I adopted a new philosophy: "If it works for me, it's meant to be". My new philosophy enabled me to do things I wouldn't do before and behave in ways I didn't consider acceptable.

My rebellious attitude mirrored my inner turmoil; I fought with my partners every time I felt bossed around, and my bad-boy attitude morphed into an unbearable trait. I wanted to make a relationship last more than anything, but something prevented me from reaching the next level.

Moving from childhood trauma to romantic relationships, I spotted the pattern. My history with abuse influenced my approach to romantic relationships. While authority figures no longer pressured me to do things, the inner critic never rested. Each time I reacted in an undesirable way, I felt worthless and worked harder to earn approval, but it seldom worked.

The pain of each breakup incremented my low self-esteem, and with time, I learned to tolerate mistreatment to avoid loneliness. My ingrained coping mechanisms led me to tolerate a high level of negativity. I brushed off insults and confrontations as stress or fatigue on my partner's part, rather than looking at myself for the cause of their distress. I had experienced the taste of abuse and of abandonment and preferred the former to avoid the later.

My childhood training prepared, or perhaps preconditioned me, to face disappointment and pain with those closest to me. Moving from place to place made me leave friends and family behind, but nothing compared to failing in love. I endured my first divorce at 25, without a circle of support, and promised myself never to repeat those mistakes.

Throughout the relationship, I had fantasized about the greener grass on the other side. But once my ignorance pushed me across the street, the pain and challenges of the relationship seemed trivial compared to the Herculean task of overcoming a heartbreak. I realized that two partners could work out all issues and that nothing justified reaching such deplorable state.

During my second marriage, I kept myself on the hook. I remembered the suffering I caused myself and resolved to see this marriage through no matter what. No pressing circumstance, job, lustful affair, or self-centered hobby would tear me away from what I wanted most. And with two kids to love and care for, failure was not an option.

But time proved me wrong, and after 7 years, we divorced due to "irreconcilable differences." We drifted apart and fell back on old patterns in moments of stress. Our arguments became self-righteous fits, leading to instances of excessive aggression and hate.

Despite these challenges, I not once thought of ending the relationship. Our kids had just turned 3 and 5, and I believed that time could heal all wounds and that we'd see eye to eye someday. But that day never arrived.

One fateful day, after a sleepless night at the hospital with the kids, our final argument broke out at home. The lack of sleep and stress from the previous night affected both of us, turning an avoidable argument into our last stand.

We fought, hurling the worst insults we could think of at each other. I grabbed my clothes to leave for work, but the situation worsened, and the police intervened. Within a few hours, I found myself on the street, with only my work clothes and nowhere to turn.

I called the three people in my favorites, but no one picked up. Stripped of dignity and support in that moment, I confronted the raw intensity of my emotions. The situation was more than I had ever encountered, and the prospect of my family dissolving tore me apart. The years of hard work, sacrifice and beating myself had only given me a taste of what I wanted, and then it disappeared. I broke down on the side of the road and sobbed uncontrollably for an hour.

After this violent argument, I understood that emotional pain surpassed any other type of suffering. Hundreds of physical beatings had left few visible scars, but the guilt, hopelessness, and feeling of inadequacy cut deeper than anything else. No number of punishing workouts, extreme sports, martial arts or toughening up had helped me manage the pain inside.

Time and again, I ignored my better judgment, buried my emotions, and justified my choices out of fear. During childhood, I concealed bruises and lied, fearing others would know what happened to me. In relationships, I often endured abuse to prevent a fight that might end in a breakup.

Despite the constant presence of my inner rational voice, I had silenced it for too long, succumbing to fears, insecurities, and impulses. After my second divorce, layoff, covid quarantine, and my new role as a mom and dad, I realized I couldn't continue in the same way.

It became clear that emotional pain could last a lifetime, no matter how tough you believe you are, and my internal struggles started to affect my relationship with my children. If I continued to listen to the inner critic, things would remain the same, or most likely, worsen.

I also recognized that my years of pent-up resentment, labels, and pain surfaced when I became angry. It took just two instances of losing my cool to understand that I made others feel the way I had felt, and that I had to change. To change my results, I had to change my routine, which pushed me to test new routines until something worked.

Integrating meditation into my routine became the first step in the right direction. I needed a method to delay my reactive responses and provide an opportunity for better decision-making. Once meditation became a regular practice, I began identifying old traumas, triggers, and ways to transform them into positive outcomes.

Reconnecting with my inner voice over time, I began my healing journey. I retrained the inner critic to serve as a coach and practiced patience with myself. This process allowed me to reflect on past behaviors and understand the long-term effects of constantly toughing it out. I also reconciled with those I felt hurt me, understanding from the offender's perspective how one can act impulsively without thinking. By understanding others had hurt me due to ignorance, not evil, I was able to shed the burden of resentment and find peace.

I recognized that, even though my upbringing had conditioned me to believe men shouldn't show vulnerability, acknowledging my own experiences with abuse proved crucial to my healing. Accepting that others had hurt me – and most importantly, my unconscious – wasn't a sign of weakness but a step forward in my journey.

This hidden path revealed a way to reconnect with my more sensitive side, the side that cherishes joy, fulfillment, and peace. I understood, through experience, the pain of abuse, both as a victim and as someone who unintentionally caused it. I recognized the inherent innocence in everyone and pledged to heal that inner child.

My journey taught me the importance of self-awareness and emotional intelligence. I prioritized exploring new ways to feel and experience, rather than avoiding and detaching. I started to live in the present, actively seeking growth opportunities, rather than fearing or hiding from the past. Although I had crafted an armor against the dragon of abuse, shedding it allowed the beast to calcinate me, so I could start anew.

XVII.

From Wreck to Reconnect: Reigniting the Fire of Passion

"We come to love not by finding a perfect person, but by learning to see an imperfect person perfectly." - Sam Keen

Why do some patterns haunt us, persistently shadowing our every step? For years, the desire to find the one-and-only drove my every choice, unravelling potential 'forever' within weeks. My need for affection put anyone who treated me decently on a pedestal, while my behavior driven by that need scared them away. The cycle of infatuation, realization, and heartbreak had become evident, resulting in emotional suffering. A divorce at 25 accentuated this pain, pushing me into a punishing journey.

But before I held myself as the prime suspect, I became convinced that relationships were destined to fail, and adopted a "better off alone" attitude. Instead of contemplating how my actions contributed to my failures, I blamed others and external circumstances. The frustration of not finding the recipe for a thriving relationship stirred feelings of hopelessness. My life had lost its meaning, and my drive to find the key to sustainable love disappeared.

After my divorce, I channeled my self-hate through dating, extreme sports, and living a superficial social media life. My last stunt was buying a motocross bike and racing, which resulted in a torn ACL. I spent days prostrated in bed, immobilized by a brace, pain killers, and despair. Thus far, I had kept myself entertained to avoid being alone, or thinking about a few weeks back, when I still had a wife and something to live for. But this motorcycle accident rendered me motionless, leaving me with nothing but time to reflect on my actions.

Without my partner or a circle of support, I rescinded to pluck into my memories for keys to my pain. I endured recovery on my own, completing tasks on one foot, including driving my manual transmission car. To increase the level of difficulty, I stopped taking the prescribed pain medication. Anytime I began to feel comfortable, I questioned my existence and reasons to continue. Physical pain paled in comparison to the torment that came when my life got quiet.

Within 3 days of surgery, I started physical therapy. I first noticed the shapeless limb I had known for my leg. My muscles had dissolved, and I had zero control over it. Much like my recent separation, losing control of my leg took me hard by surprise. My leg did not respond to my mental command, and within a few seconds, I envisioned the negative impact on my life.

Before I freaked out, however, I asked the therapist about my issue. After chuckling due to my scared face, he told me I experienced what's called atrophy. When muscles are not used due to injury or surgery, they weaken and shrink in size. My injured leg reflected the decay in my personal life. The burdening situation annoyed me but also shone a light upon my problems.

What if, like muscles, lack of maintenance lead to relationship atrophy? In the past, once familiarity seemed to set in, I felt accomplished and took my partners for granted. The dates and romance waned in proportion to how comfortable I grew within the relationship. While I thought that working hard and giving my partner luxuries proved my love, I had failed to nurture her mind and heart, focusing too much on material possessions or appearances.

How had I veered so far off the path? The dots connected one by one, starting with my dedication to jobs, cars, and maintaining a certain image. I had neglected the well-being oh the person that mattered most by prioritizing other, less important things that fed my ego. It wasn't the number of things I did for my her, but how I made her feel that counted most.

Identifying the problem allowed me to find solutions and get closer to my goal. If muscles could be rebuilt, so could emotional connections. My leg had become useless after sustained abuse and a traumatic experience, not overnight. This meant that the inevitable ending I feared could be avoided early on, by attending to the responsibilities I assumed when bringing someone else into my life.

Over 13 years helped me practice until I adopted this perspective for good. My current relationship lost some flair after a couple of years together, but instead of the fear of capsizing, I accepted the challenge.

From that point on, I planned weekly dates or a new activity, despite our years together. The fear of repeating past mistakes pushed me to become the best partner I could be. If I wanted a chance at enjoying a sustainable relationship, I needed to make my partner feel the way I made her feel when I wanted her more than anything; loved, valued, understood, and cared for.

Getting to date my partner again became an unexpected gift. I got to explore new places and feel the rush of falling in love with someone I knew and trusted. Love, passion, and fulfillment only needed to be nurtured to grow. Better than a new relationship, understanding that the power of falling in love resided within my perspective freed me from fear, and the same destructive cycle.

I shifted my focus to improving our emotional well-being and ensuring her core needs were covered. My ignorance and self-centered behavior had led to chaos in the past, so I turned to new perspectives to help me engrain the change. Learning to appreciate and making my partner feel like in the beginning became the winning key in preventing love atrophy.

Creating a strong relationship takes time, but the emotional home of trust and understanding are worth the effort. Love, in its essence, is an ever-evolving dance. Looking back, I realized that I moved to the music without knowing the steps, but I now held the key to one of my biggest fears. I learned to put my chips were they matter and treat my partner the way I did in the beginning, so I don't worry about the end.

XVIII.

The Dichotomy of Defiance: Understanding True Respect

"I care not what others think of what I do, but I care very much about what I think of what I do. That is character!" - Theodore Roosevelt

---

My father's backhand landed on my mouth before I could mutter an explanation. I stumbled backward, my lips bleeding and throbbing from the impact. "You are going to respect me!" he growled through clenched teeth, deeply engraving in me the consequences of disrespecting someone.

In school, teachers reprimanded me for doodling or talking after finishing my tasks, and they often involved my parents, which only aggravated my behavior. As the years went by, the severity of the consequences for insubordination escalated, fueling my resentment towards any form of authority.

In the realm of love and relationships, my hardened attitude became an invisible barrier. Accustomed to living defensively, I instinctively learned to say no first, then ask questions. Years of compromising my feelings and well-being brewed a resentment that became difficult to hide. What started as a docile child morphed into an uptight, demanding, and frequently angry adult.

Although this persona emerged from self-preservation, it brought more heartaches than security. My "macho-man" façade camouflaged my own ignorance and insecurities, pushing away those I deeply cared for. I soon grasped the destructive nature of this defensive stance. Demanding apologies only bred resentment, straining already fragile bonds, and pushing relationships closer to an irreparable rift.

In my quest for answers and new perspectives, I recognized the need to embrace vulnerability. Although my past was riddled with instances of people misconstruing my kindness for weakness, I believed that shedding my emotional weapons could pave a path forward.

Eager to redefine my understanding of respect, especially in romantic relationships, I dissected its antonym: disrespect. This exercise exposed my behavioral patterns. What had begun as a shield for my emotional well-being had transformed into a reactive, often dismissive attitude, alienating those around me.

To rectify this pattern, I redirected my focus. I practiced self-compassion, eliminating self-criticism, and silencing the burdensome voices of doubt. I realized I'd been held back by the fear of romantic failures and decided to let my inner voice guide my actions.

For far too long, I lived under the shadow of others' expectations, sidelining my own instincts and emotions. But no matter how much I sacrificed, I couldn't influence their actions. This paradigm shift catalyzed my healing and reinforced my belief in my unique identity. While we all have our individual quirks and strengths, I came to understand that our core emotions and needs are universally shared.

The weight of past regrets became the fuel for my evolution. Years of introspection and experiences illuminated the true essence of respect, enabling me to avoid past pitfalls and spare me future mistakes.

With deep gratitude, I now recognize the importance of emotions in shaping our lives and the foundational principle of mutual respect. Having never experienced true respect, I had been ensnared by misguided notions of its nature. I once believed respect was born of admiration or fear, but my journey proved otherwise.

True respect emerged when I viewed others through the lens of shared human experiences, acknowledging their battles, heartaches, and triumphs. To see others the way I saw myself; another person fighting a silent battle and having to put one foot in front of another without really knowing why. This realization instilled in me the need to shed my judgements and misconceptions about respect, and extend it to anyone sharing this journey.

By embracing mutual respect, I've seen its power nurture not only my loved one's emotional growth but also deepen my own understanding. Respect has firmly rooted itself as an unwavering pillar in my moral compass. If I've grown and healed so deeply by valuing others, imagine the world we could shape by practicing this daily.

I believe that the solution for our inner turmoil is living the Golden Rule, and realizing that what we do to others, we inevitably do to ourselves. The punishment, however, is often worse than the crime, emotional suffering. So why start? The moment I began respecting others for who they are, and not who I considered them to be, I experienced the acceptance and respect from others, but most important, myself.

XIX.

Ambers of Gold: Lighting the Path to True Romance

"Romance is the glamour which turns the dust of everyday life into a golden haze." - Elinor Glyn

From childhood crushes to profound adult relationships, my journey has been a winding path through the realms of love and its challenges. A concept hidden in plain sight, I grappled with the meaning of 'romance' only after a series of colorful experiences.

My early steps into the world of affection were elementary. Eager for acknowledgment or a simple smile from classmates, I showed my interest through drawings, paper flowers, and love notes. I still remember, with a hint of mischief, using the teacher's chalk to write love notes for a young crush. Those were simpler times, filled with innocent gestures of young affection.

I went on my first date at 18, having just moved to the U.S. My downstairs neighbor and his girlfriend invited me on a double date with her cousin. Terrified to go, I excused myself, citing work or other responsibilities. However, my neighbor, recognizing my apprehension, peer-pressured me into accepting.

The date was a disaster. When I opened the car door for her, all three burst into laughter. What my grandparents had taught me about being a gentleman seemed ridiculous, and the only people I knew made fun of me for it. My heart plummeted. Each laugh felt like a stab, questioning not just my gesture but my entire approach to romance. I retreated into silence for the entire 20-minute ride home.

With time and practice, the once innocent romantic gestures began to feel out of place, even outdated. Facing rejection and sometimes ridicule, I started withholding my emotions, constructing a protective layer that obscured the essence of true romance.

As I continued dating, I faced the same challenges. Girls seemed more interested in guys who acted tough or ignored them, whereas I tried to emulate the protagonists of romantic movies. The approach that initially seemed promising had become my Achilles heel; I had become the nice guy who finished last.

Challenging my string of disappointments, I began to question the very nature of romance. Questions brewed within me: Was romance overrated? Was it just about going with the flow, without becoming emotional entangled? Did I have to ride a black horse and serenade my partners at midnight?

This introspection led me to a phase where dating felt like a numbers game rather than the pursuit of genuine connections. To seek answers, I experimented by dating a variety of women, adopting different approaches. Recognizing the slim chances of a lasting relationship, I forsook my tried-and-true methods in favor of exploring unfamiliar territories.

Through this journey, I realized a crucial lesson: At its core, romance is about intention, thought, and genuine emotion. The thrill of new encounters proved unsustainable in the long run. Gifts and sugar rushes were momentary satisfactions, but romance entailed embracing affection, intimacy, and emotional connection. Any thoughtful gesture that could make my partner feel loved and cared for.

Contrary to my earlier beliefs, I didn't need grand gestures like hiring a mariachi band or planning extravagant trips. The whispered endearments, stolen gazes, and intimate moments that bridge two souls became the epitome of romantic behavior for me. Addressing my partner as *love* or *gorgeous*, kissing her gently, or *I miss you* texts captured the essence of the emotional connection we both yearned for.

It took a myriad of experiences, both highs and lows, to fathom the pivotal role of romance in a thriving relationship. Choosing love, recognizing, and cherishing small moments amidst life's challenges became my axiom. While I had mistaken kindness and romance for weakness, proving myself wrong unveiled a hidden cove of peace and fulfillment.

Whether it's admiring the way my partner tends to our garden or watching her play with our 7 dogs, I've learned to value our shared moments and express gratitude through heartfelt romantic gestures. Simple acts, like flowers, a quiet gaze, or a bear-shaped notes hold the power to fortify our bond. In these subtle expressions, I've come to understand that the path to true romance is not about grand gestures, but about the authenticity of the heart and the magical moments we share.

XX.

Dragon's Gaze: The Unmasking of Red Flags

"The greatest happiness is to know the source of unhappiness." - Fyodor Dostoevsky.

———————◆◆◆◆———————

Just as a road sign warns of upcoming hazards, red flags in relationships are instinctual alerts of potential pitfalls. Whether in school, work or relationships, this sense of unease emerged whenever something clashed with my values or emotions. However, I'd grown accustomed to dismissing it as just a state of mind.

In my younger years, I was immersed in an environment where dishonesty and aggression were daily realities. My intuition had frequently signaled danger, yet circumstances often left me with no choice but to forge ahead. These early trials cultivated an overconfidence in my decision-making, leading me to underestimate potential risks.

Within relationships, I felt uneasy about my partners' minor deceits or inconsistencies. My initiation into heartbreak came at 18, when my girlfriend declared her love for me only to leave for another guy the very next day. For weeks, I had felt something didn't make sense, but attributed it to my own insecurities. But my intuition had been right, and this betrayal imprinted upon me the need for constant vigilance against further deception.

My approach worked for some time, until his heightened state of alertness wore me down. I began to interpret every small discrepancy as a major warning. Relationships became a tightrope walk of anxiety and suspicion, filled with flags that stirred my fears. Instead of facing these concerns head-on, I hid behind a facade of jealousy and faux confidence. These repressed insecurities surfaced in more destructive ways, such as passive-aggressive comments or behavior.

By marking every partner as potentially untrustworthy, I set myself up for failure. That initial heartbreak left an indelible mark, but I needed to let that fear go. It took many relationships and two divorces to surrender and learn the true meaning of red flags.

Looking back, it was clear my fears painted these flags with a thick brush of impending doom. Memories of past betrayals made me instinctively brace for future hurts, setting up a self-fulfilling prophecy. The specter of past traumas magnified my current anxieties. I misinterpreted situations, becoming defensive rather than introspective. This instinct to shield my heart led to blame, accusations, and emotional distance, ironically causing the very breakups I feared.

Unraveling these patterns lifted a massive burden off my chest. I had approached current relationships through the lens of past traumas, assuming before asking. Simple actions or comments from partners shouldn't have created inner turmoil. Yet they did, due to unresolved inner issues, not because of anything they did wrong.

Most of these red flags were more reflective of my own insecurities than any issues with my partner. Instead of signifying imminent danger, they served as cues for introspection and improvement. Were these genuine concerns or echoes of past fears?

While some flags did highlight legitimate concerns, addressing them with vulnerability and understanding, rather than suspicion, became the key to transformation. Love isn't about building walls; it's about tearing them down. My walls, built from insecurities, burdened my soul, and blocked me from the connection I sought.

Throughout this introspective journey, red flags morphed from threats to growth indicators. They spotlighted areas within me that needed care and healing. I came to realize that the most formidable challenges aren't with others but with our own inner demons. Overcoming them led to the connection I had longed for, helping me overcome my fears, and become the person my loved ones needed.

Red flags, when properly recognized, don't spell disaster; they mark opportunities for growth. They remind us that while it's easy to blame others, introspection is the real game-changer. In love, challenges are won by understanding ourselves, not by fending off imagined threats. If red flags are reflections of our internal struggles, isn't it more productive to face our fears than to place blame on our partners?

XXI.

Imaginary Shackles: The Shadows of Paranoia

"I am not afraid of tomorrow, for I have seen yesterday and I love today." –
William Allen White

In the past, societal expectations and my own insecurities allowed paranoia to blur the lines of personal privacy. Whenever that nagging feeling arose, instead of confronting by talking to my partner, I dove into imagined scenarios and obsessive jealousy. Each time I crossed those personal boundaries, like scrolling through my partner's messages, the discoveries weren't revelations of betrayal but rather reflections of my own mistrust.

This cycle, driven by the fear of betrayal, offered temporary relief but planted seeds of deeper issues. Guilt and shame weighed me down after every instance, eroding the very foundation of trust in the relationship. And when the weight of guilt became unbearable, I faced the consequences of my actions, often feeling lost and isolated.

Being trapped in a cycle of jealousy and suspicion became tiresome. Sleepless nights of anxious thoughts led to wasted time I could've spent with my partner. It was like hustling a second job alongside my regular life, always being on the lookout, questioning my partner's every move.

This mindset, a combination of anxiety and deceit, became a heavy burden. The toll my behavior took on the relationship never justified the "secrets" uncovered, or the painful places it led.

Then the tables turned. For the first time in my life, I dated someone who valued me and scared other women away. Finding myself on the receiving end, at first, felt like concern masked as protective gestures. But those gestures soon morphed into a suffocating shadow. Being constantly under scrutiny, I felt cornered and misunderstood. Each unwarranted accusation chipped away at my confidence, making me question my worth and decisions, fearful of being misinterpreted.

From being someone cherished, I became the only suspect in an endless series of imaginary crimes. Each accusation left me feeling powerless, and I did my best to prove my partner wrong. I gave up parts of my identity, like friendships and hobbies, to make her feel secure. But nothing worked.

Years of walking on eggshells took their toll, both on me and the relationship. The incessant need to prove myself became exhausting. Boundaries seemed essential. I understood that love shouldn't come with the price tag of constant surveillance or self-compromise.

My partner's approach had obliterated any credibility in myself, as well as my desire to prove myself any further. While the losses of this breakup represented everything I had, if I kept on the same path, I wouldn't have anything left.

This experience underscored the value of genuine transparency. If suspicion arose, confronting my own insecurities became the path forward, not clandestine investigations. I realized that for a relationship to truly flourish, it needed to be built on mutual trust, respect, and open dialogue.

When faced with the fiery dragon of my fears, I challenged myself to confront and overcome the limiting beliefs that held me captive. Transparency became a beacon, guiding me towards a relationship where personal privacy is cherished and encouraged, not trespassed.

I also adopted a more vulnerable stance, asking my partner when something didn't make sense. Most times than not, my fears and negative experiences had created ghosts in my head, harmless paper dragons. Experience taught me that relationships where one feels judged and evaluated can quickly crumble. It took many unpleasant moments for me to grasp the importance of privacy and its role in nurturing trust.

From that point, transparency and privacy became axioms in my life. To truly understand and be understood by my partner, I had to prioritize open dialogue over secretive investigations. My new approach encouraged open communication and mutual resolution. The more we felt heard, the better we handled challenges as a team, until our trust obliterated the shadow of fear.

With time and patience, we built a system of trust and honesty. I came to understand how my past actions had affected others, emphasizing the importance of trust and privacy in everyone's life. Embracing the real, unaltered image of my partner, rather than the distorted version painted by fear, set the foundation for a sustainable and fulfilling relationship.

Trust became a sword against the beast, and with it, I chased away the serpents of doubt.

As I matured, prioritizing trust and privacy became non-negotiable. Lessons from the past shaped my present, enabling me to cultivate a relationship where we understood and valued each other's individuality. Trusting my partner meant letting go of the need to control, creating a foundation where love thrived on mutual respect and honesty.

XXII.

Unveiling the Hydra's Lair: The Four Heads of the Beast

"Fortis Fortuna Adiuvat" – Terence

Arguments, in my experience, are an unavoidable and necessary ingredient of a successful relationship. However, I believed that fights and disagreements meant ruining my chances with the possible love of my life. The idea of screaming and cursing at each other had nothing to do with my vision of love.

As a kid, I witnessed my dad stonewall or leave when my mom nagged him, often threatening to never come back. During a car ride home from my aunt's house, he got out of the car mid-journey and walked 10 miles home. On another occasion, the police were involved, and he left for a couple of days.

These situations imprinted in me the need to avoid conflict, and therefore situations of abandonment. I witnessed my mother suffer every time he behaved this way, while I experienced the fear of the unknown along with my siblings.

In work and relationships, the same principle seemed to apply. I have been dumped and fired for standing my ground. It seemed that arguments were an omen for pain, and I would do anything to avoid them, even if it meant dancing on burning coals.

In my first marriage, avoiding arguments became crucial. Each time we fought, one of us ended up in tears, hurt and withdrawn. While we patched up and moved forward one way or another, nothing could undo the damage already caused. Besides anger and confusion,

I had failed to recognize my mistakes, leading to shame, and forced apologies.

Although a shallow "I'm sorry" relieved the tension in the air, the lingering feelings of resentment became difficult to ignore. As familiarity and contempt grew, we found enough flaws in each other to fall into the "irreconcilable differences" category at the age of 25.

Getting divorced at such a young age became a nightmare I didn't foresee, and I wondered if marriage was a once-in-a-lifetime thing. I had failed at the ultimate commitment, which shattered my self-confidence, self-worth, and hope. My reasons to live became blurry, my confusion grew, and I spiraled downward into the abyss of self-loathing and hate.

The constant replay of the times I messed up beat me to a pulp. Time showed that most issues were trivial and preventable by small changes. The excruciating pain of destroying the "happily ever after" I had imagined, taught me that arguments were better handled with love, patience, and as a team, not against each other. Unless I wanted to build a relationship again and end up in the same place.

While I didn't know exactly how to make this happen, I resolved to find a way to overcome arguments; otherwise, marriage would be nothing more than a sugar-coated emotional prison.

A year of research and error led me to The Gottman Institute's website, where I stumbled upon an article that changed my life. This article, written by Ellie Lisitsa, delved into Dr. John Gottman's research of the biggest predictors of divorce: The Four Horsemen of The Apocalypse.

According to Dr. Gottman, the Four Horsemen are Criticism, Defensiveness, Contempt, and Stonewalling. These were the same traits I had identified in our arguments but could not put my finger on. It became clear to me that I had developed these defensive tactics as a way of dealing with threats, the unknown, and my deepest fears.

Equipped with ways to differentiate these destructive traits in my behavior, I embarked on taking them down one by one. My journey didn't unfold overnight, but practice and resilience allowed me to eradicate these poisons from my life and reap the ultimate rewards.

Let's delve into how I slew them, one by one.

XXIII.

Slaying Criticism: The First Battle in Relationship Renewal

"When you judge another, you do not define them, you define yourself." - Wayne Dyer

---

Growing up, I often found myself on the receiving end of critical remarks, highlighting my inability to meet others' expectations. It felt as though I consistently missed the mark, my failures intensified by criticism instead of understanding. These early experiences shaped how I interacted with others, including romantic partners. Despite my efforts to change, the criticism seemed relentless, leading me to believe that finding lasting love was impossible.

How did I reach this bleak conclusion? Whether as a son, student, worker, or romantic partner, I always fell short. Years of molding myself to others' expectations had left me both angry and empty-handed.

In response, I began to lash out, learning to argue and counter with aggression. Though I gained a new level of self-confidence, it was rooted in ego and self-righteousness. I used to tolerate abuse and accusations to avoid punishment or a breakup, but now I confronted others head-on, convinced I had nothing to lose. This defensive behavior became ingrained in me, turning me into the very criticizer I had once feared.

When things didn't go my way in relationships, I used phrases like you never, why can't you? or you always? My past failures had supposedly taught me the right ways to handle situations, and I couldn't see beyond my own perspective. I pointed out every improvement my partners should consider and unconsciously expected compliance. When reality didn't meet my expectations, resentment set in, leading to increased conflict and the eventual end of many relationships.

I had known the power of criticism since childhood, painfully aware of what it felt like to never be good enough. The desperate child in me cried out for approval; my angrier side grew more resentful with each rejection. Yet, here I was, treating my loved ones the same way, thinking I was helping them improve.

Once I opened my eyes to the aftermath of criticism, I realized that my approach had become a self-defeating cycle. If criticism had caused me anger and anxiety, why would others feel any differently? I had instilled in them the feelings of insufficiency and inadequacy that I so dreaded.

After my second divorce, I compared relationships to building a home. A complaint resembled a leak in the roof, something to be repaired rather than railed against. Criticizing my partner was like hammering a hole through her self-esteem wall, a destructive act that could never truly be repaired.

When criticism surfaced in my current relationship, I recognized old patterns and adopted a new approach. Instead of demanding change, I offered help and managed issues with love, support, and genuine concern for my partner's well-being. This new behavior alleviated our emotional burden and allowed her to feel loved and supported. With time, criticism gave way to gratitude, and our relationship blossomed.

Changing my inner dialogue helped me heal. It also helped me shed criticism and replace it with positive reinforcement. Once I stopped tyrannizing myself, I saw no need in holding others to the same expectation, and emotional pain.

This transformation brought peace to my heart and changed my view of the world. I stopped measuring others by my expectations and only offered my opinion when asked. Criticism became a tool for growth rather than a stumbling block, no longer undermining the foundation of my relationships.

And instead of fighting others when criticized, I welcomed all opinions as tips I should at least listen to. My results proved I had much to learn, and why not listen to those that see what I can't? Most times than not, I have discovered an angle that saved me pain and suffering. Worst case scenario? I'm thankful to others for telling me things they think would help me improve. Win-win.

XXIV.

Facing the Fire: Conquering the Beast of Defensiveness

"I'm not afraid of storms, for I am learning how to sail my ship." - Louisa
May Alcott

As a kid, I felt the need to stay vigilant and sharp. Those around me had shown me the pain they could inflict, and I wanted to avoid it at all costs. Sometimes the pain was physical; other times, it was mental or emotional. My dad would react first when angry at me, ask questions later, and then destroy things I cherished.

In high school, the three guys I hung out with accused me of stealing a wallet to cover their tracks at my expense. Their accusations led to weekly visits from the school counselor and nearly resulted in my expulsion.

On another occasion, my dad discovered my hidden collection of Metallica cassette tapes and Spawn comic books. Without giving me a chance to explain, he accused me of worshipping the devil and burned my treasured belongings in our mud oven.

I experienced the same pattern in friendships, jobs, and relationships. People close to me had no issues putting their interests before mine. Years of encountering this issue evoked resentment in me, resulting in angry defense mechanisms when accused or belittled by others.

Through this learned response, I crafted a shield to protect myself from blame and not feeling good enough. But this shield, instead of protecting me, only drove those I loved further away.

While my closed-off and defensive approach served me well navigating the streets on my own, it translated to poor results in relationships I cherished. The stubbornness and anger escalated fights to the worst outcomes, including separation and divorce. Feeling less than enough led to fits of self-righteous indignation, sparking anger to prove the opposite, and deteriorating our emotional state further.

To change my approach, I transmuted criticism into constructive suggestions, but I soon began to perceive them as attacks and insults. After experiencing the same outcome a few times in a row, I anticipated the outcome of the next argument and reacted before asking questions. Nothing had changed in the last six episodes, so I instigated the change inside myself. I assumed my partner's intentions before they were fully expressed, and this led me to act out my emotions.

The pain in my loved ones' eyes every time I lashed out still haunts me, a stark reminder of how destructive my defensiveness had become. By reacting before asking, I deprived my loved ones of a proper defense or at least the benefit of the doubt.

Assuming their intentions were spiteful and shielding myself from their attacks only pulled to pieces what could have been a beautiful relationship. My own perception of events led me to respond as-if, robbing myself to give the situation a different interpretation.

This realization was painful to come to terms with, but it provided me with another key piece in the puzzle of arguments. I could clearly see how I had played the biggest role in my own downfall, and how the guilt I had placed on others was mine to carry.

This lesson motivated me to change my approach, and consequently, my destination.

When it came to solving relationship challenges, being defensive offered me no advantage, no leverage. It only added to the problem. One situation, however, changed my approach for good.

On a summer afternoon, my partner complained about something I had said. Her accusation instilled in me the need to bear arms, grinding my teeth and clenching my fist while she laid it on me. But instead of reacting, I detached, listened, and asked her to elaborate.

For the first time in a relationship, I had shut down the voice of defensiveness and had become open to hearing my partner. The understanding that followed became a revelation. Within a few minutes, I learned about blind behaviors that could have ended in tragic outcomes.

Our conversation became a dialogue instead of a battle, a safe martial arts practice rather than a street fight.

Taming the beast of defensiveness allowed others, especially my partner and children, to have a voice in how they wanted to be treated. Their suggestions didn't mean they loved me less or that I wasn't good enough; they gave me more tools and options to help and grow.

This realization changed my inner dialogue and perspective, bypassing the need to protect myself. If my partner became defensive during an argument, I switched from opponent to teammate, focusing on our mutual goal. This subtle shift turned destructive arguments into a stronger push in the right direction.

With time and practice, I learned to not only accept criticism but actively seek it to improve my life and relationships. I ask for my family's perspective and opinion, and their wisdom has never disappointed. The ultimate prize for defeating defensiveness is not just feeling better; it's earning trust from those I love, using my sword of experience to slay my bad habits and blind spots.

The journey to overcome defensiveness taught me more than I ever anticipated. It wasn't just about laying down my guard or avoiding conflict. It unveiled a pathway to understanding, empathy, and, most importantly, growth.

Like the careful mending of a fragile piece of art, I learned to handle my relationships with care, knowing that the strongest connections are often the ones most nurtured. If I find myself digging in my heels, I remember: The weapons we use to protect ourselves often become the prisons that hold us hostage.

I chose to drop them, and discovered freedom in vulnerability, trust, and love. Contrary to decades-old beliefs, letting down my defenses did not make me weak; it made me stronger, more compassionate, and helped me open the gates to the emotional abundance I sought.

XXV.

Taming Contempt: The Hydra's Third Menace

"Contempt is the weapon of the weak and a defense against one's own despised and unwanted feelings." - Alice Miller

---

The first time I encountered the essence of contempt, it unveiled a hidden connection threading through every person I knew. As a child navigating the streets of South America, conflict was an unyielding presence. Aggressors were omnipresent, leaving no escape but to confront danger head-on. My years of enduring taunts and brawls wore down my resolve, but the bitterness remained. My redemption came in an unexpected guise: the mastery of contempt.

A derisive sneer, a disdainful chuckle, an aloof look – these gestures became more powerful than any verbal attack or intimidation. The hurt I could cause without uttering a single word ended confrontations that I had long struggled with. Contempt grew beyond a mere defense; it evolved into a core part of my identity, a subtle game of supremacy that I played with finesse.

In the sphere of love, this game infiltrated impassioned disputes. Contempt became my tool, revealing itself in dismissive actions, condescending pet names, and an aura of self-imposed greatness. Believing that I solidified the bonds of love, I was, instead, tearing them apart.

Upon the heartbreaking end of my first marriage, I saw the reflection of a man marred by contempt. My strongest card had become a destructive force, steadily eroding the relationships I cherished most. Contempt had ceased to be a defensive reaction; it had become a feature of my very character, trait that ensured more suffering that peace.

The journey to overcome this deeply rooted behavior proved slow and complex. I grappled with apprehension, obstinacy, and an ingrained need to affirm my self-worth. Change required self-reflection, acknowledgment of my imperfections, and the bravery to welcome vulnerability. But most important, I had to find a way to stop myself before unsheathing contempt again.

I also need to destroy the shield I had carefully constructed, leaving myself bare and susceptible. Though fraught with doubt and concerned that others might take advantage of my newfound openness, I stumbled upon an unknown stream of fulfillment and peace, the water in the desert.

As I peeled away the layers of contempt, a remarkable transformation began to take shape. Relationships blossomed in unimaginable ways, nourished by mutual respect, empathy, and sincere connection. I found tranquility within myself, a delightful peace that dwarfed the fleeting satisfaction of winning an argument.

Contempt had once been both my weapon and armor, but it had turned on me, leaving scars that only time and wisdom could heal. Rising above it signaled more than a triumph; it remade me, allowing me to see others not as adversaries but as fellow travelers, each wrestling with their unique fears, hopes, and dreams.

Although challenging at best, facing the beasts that tormented me became the most rewarding journey. I have learned that contempt, though powerful, yields hollow victories, and years of pain. In its place, I've unearthed a more profound, genuine way of connecting with others and myself.

In the end, contempt became a deceptive ally, a seductive force promising strength but delivering loneliness and regret. By acknowledging its destructive potential and choosing a road of empathy, understanding, and modesty, I forged fulfilling, sustainable, and joyful relationships with myself and those I love. The third head of the hydra had been tamed, and I had one to go.

XXVI.

Breaking the Spell: The End of Stonewalling

"The walls we build around us to keep out the sadness also keep out the joy."
- Jim Rohn

———————◄•••►———————

The first instance of stonewalling I observed was my dad, biting his lips for a solid 10 minutes while my mom reprimanded him. When he had had enough, he abruptly stopped the car, abandoned the driver's seat, and walked over 10 miles to get home. This dramatic event, and the lingering echoes it left behind, marked a turning point in how I perceived conflict.

Although this was the first time I witnessed stonewalling, it wasn't the last. This too-common trait became a staple in every conflict. I had seen my close relatives, neighbors and even friends walk away when saturated by anger. In my case, I stonewalled as a way of holding my sadness, anger, and explosive frustration inside when punished, humiliated or hurt.

Unconsciously absorbing this trait, I began to adopt stonewalling at an early age. Driven by my dad's disciplinary methods, the fear was drummed out of me, and rather than beg or explain myself, I learned to bite my tongue and endure the punishment stoically. Maybe – I thought – if I didn't show weakness, he would cease. But my silence only escalated the severity of the punishments, and I grew resilient in parallel.

In my adult life, stonewalling morphed into a recurring pattern in my romantic endeavors. I can recall the moment in my first long-term relationship when I stonewalled for the very first time. What started as minor disagreements quickly escalated into ultimatums. My partner's defensiveness frustrated me to no end, and while I sought to clear myself of any accusations, my resolve crumbled. Stonewalling became my refuge, my way to ward off the explosive arguments and resist reciprocating the blows.

Yet, in time, this defensive posture carved a vast chasm between us, transforming our once-blooming relationship into a barren wasteland. We were strangers, cohabiting but disconnected, all because I chose evasion over resolution.

The true reckoning came in the wake of my second divorce, a stark and undeniable testament that stonewalling was a dead-end street. During disputes, stonewalling became my last bastion after fruitless attempts at peace and fending off inaccurate accusations. The resentment I felt gnawed at my soul incessantly, even as I avoided the bigger fights.

To forge a healthy relationship, I had to slay the dragon of stonewalling and discover constructive ways to handle conflicts. The epiphany struck me hard: my silence was not a fortress but a prison. It was a way to sidestep conflict at the high price of authentic connections and emotional vitality. Though I had spared myself the immediate pain of regret, withdrawing emotionally wreaked havoc within my mind and heart. How many potential bridges had I destroyed in the pursuit of self-preservation?

Overcoming stonewalling meant facing my fears head-on. If in the past I unplugged from a fight to avoid further escalation — which seldom worked —, I now had to see the fight through and, somehow, find peace in the end.

To achieve my goal, I needed to dissect what frightened me, be it humiliation or yet another failed relationship. If I acted in such radical way, it had to be for a radical reason; to avoid experiencing the pain of abandonment again. But decades of the same approach yielded opposite results, and the need for a new approach became evident.

I found new strategies to communicate, express myself, and handle arguments with love. Instead of retreating into silence, I learned to pause, apologize, and ask my partner to rephrase her concerns. Together, we paved a new path towards resolution, one founded on mutual respect and understanding. And I discovered a tranquility and joy that came from no longer suppressing my emotions.

Changing this deeply ingrained habit resembled a wrestling match against my own shadow. Old patterns tempted me, but armed with a newfound awareness, I embraced the opportunity to transform my behavior and consequently, my life. By conquering the last head of the Hydra, I eliminated my dread of conflict and found peace at the end of the battle. Chaos became an opportunity, reshaping not only my life but also influencing those around me.

Stonewalling once seemed a refuge, a way to shield myself from the rawness of conflict. It took years to see that it was not a shield, but a barrier — a barrier that stifled growth, connection, and authentic living. The walls I once hid behind are no longer fortresses but relics of a past self. In tearing them down, I discovered the strength to confront and the wisdom to understand. My relationships are now bridges, not barriers, and in their construction, I gained the courage to truly love and live.

XXVII.

Dragon's Inferno: Betrayal's Consuming Flame

"The cave you fear to enter holds the treasure you seek." - Joseph
Campbell

Although the previous four beasts accounted for most of my failures, there is a fifth that lurks in the depths of hell: Betrayal. It slinks through the shadows of relationships, unseen and unnoticed, until it pounces with surprise, speed, and violence of action, slicing trust with surgical precision.

I felt the sting of betrayal at a young age. A promise from my father to be my mentor and friend shattered like fragile glass when he lashed out over a trivial misstep. It felt as if a piece of me had been ripped from my chest, replaced with discomfort and pain. This initial wound festered, teaching me to distrust even those closest to me, and ingraining a fear of betrayal that shaped my formative years.

By 18, I experienced my first heartbreak, a direct result of infidelity. New to the game of love, I wore my heart on my sleeve, making uncalled-for sacrifices for love. I rode the bus for hours to see her, called her every day, and showered her with gifts and attention that I couldn't afford. One afternoon, she confessed her love and commitment to me — my life-long dream come true. The very next day, however, she dumped me for someone else, and for the first time, I endured the crushing sorrow of a heartbreak.

While betrayal from friends and family was hurtful, it was not wholly unexpected. But the despair and emotional suffering of a blindsiding heartbreak, however, was something else entirely; a beast that lurked even in my sleep. From that moment on, I approached every person with a lens of paranoia and mistrust, every commitment representing a chance of being lied to or betrayed. My perception imprisoned me in a cycle of fear and anxiety, filled with endless "what ifs?"

Throughout life's ambiguous path, the dragon of betrayal terrorized me more than anything else. Death, destitution, or moving across continents meant nothing compared to the fear of losing love. Friends turned accusers; unfair terminations from work, the sorrow of infidelity; these experiences cut wide and deep, cultivating in me a sense of distrust and defensiveness.

To manage my fear, I managed my expectations, and gave nothing more than I didn't want to lose. I kept potential partners at arm's length, holding in my innermost thoughts and emotions to myself. My confident facade hid an insecure child, and having gotten burnt before, I feared getting close to the fire. This emotional gap, however, allowed for outside snakes to infiltrate and cause trouble. In a cruel twist, I found myself playing the betrayer, a role adopted out of defense in a world that taught me that trust was for the naïve.

But none of my emotional stunts yielded good results. Betraying my partner, even if only emotionally, left me feeling guilty and heavy-hearted. I loathed myself for doing to others what I feared them doing to me and experienced the same level of pain by betraying than being betrayed. Through repetitive experience and loss, I proved to myself that the invisible principle of betrayal had very real, and long lasting, consequences.

The path that led me to that realization unfolded slowly. It began with flirting with someone here, getting a number there; all fun and games to get myself out of my comfort zone. One day, however, my game turned serious, and I got a crush on someone while already committed to another. For months, my partner and I had been locked in a battle of attrition, ending up at opposite ends of the house. I felt neglected and unloved in my relationship, but this new person reignited feelings of self-worth and passion.

I attempted to pursue this affair and failed with both the new person and my partner. The new girl rejected me in anger, and my girlfriend uncovered my deception, leaving me shortly after. Although I begged and promised to change, the person I cherished left me for my dishonesty, leaving me with the embarrassing realization of my cowardice and weakness. My need for attention and validation had made betrayal my master, turning me into what I despised most.

I spent months repenting for my actions, learning what it felt like to betray someone else. It hurt as much as being betrayed, and that realization changed my life. From that moment on, I vowed to honor integrity, to become the person I wanted by my side, and to avoid the inevitable destruction of dishonest ways. Behaving properly wasn't about superstition; it was an unyielding principle, like gravity. The higher the drop, the harder the fall.

These lessons did not come easily. They arrived with withdrawal, a retreat behind walls of silence and suspicion. But part of overcoming old patterns is facing them head-on. By discovering my core driving needs, I understood the impact of my behavior and found more sustainable ways to seek what I wanted.

I devoted myself to doing my best, especially in relationships and self-development. Giving without remembering, receiving without forgetting, and honoring what I feel is true loosened the shackles of fear and insecurity. I became the partner I'd like by my side, and in turn, found the same in others.

Betrayal, I've learned, is not an obstacle but a continual challenge. As humans, we resort to unethical behavior to satisfy needs, unaware of the painful consequences. Its existence reminds us of life's twists and the importance of honesty, commitment, and integrity; principles that exist for our — and everyone's — best interest.

Nothing stays the same, and life's is a roller-coaster of uncertainty and challenges. But trust, integrity, and love can dwarf the chaos of the unknown. Knowing what to expect from those who matter most brings stability, peace, and an emotional home we don't ever want to leave.

Today, love flows untainted by doubt, and I live free from betrayal's shadow. Its harsh lessons illuminated a path to genuine relationships and untapped emotional strength. Resisting its pull liberated me from guilt and fear, shaping me into the man my loved ones needed most, especially myself.

XXVIII.

Cracking the Dragon's Egg: The Dangers of Jealousy

"The jealous are troublesome to others, but a torment to themselves."
- William Penn

Growing up in an environment of self-interest and mutual distrust, I saw jealousy's insidious effects everywhere: in my parents' relationship, among neighbors, and even in my friends' romantic lives. My father's jealousy manifested in ugly ways, as he confronted anyone who approached my mother. But he didn't just confront other men; my mom got an earful behind closed doors. This cycle repeated many times, with my dad holding my mom responsible for things out of her control under the guise of protection.

When I started dating, my father's approach became my own, perspective that destroyed my first marriage. I feigned confidence and sought to intimidate anyone close to a romantic interest. Though some praised my bad boy attitude, it masked profound distrust and a narrow view of relationships. Watching my parents' relationship unfold taught me to distrust men nearby and keep an eye on my partner, too. If I heard a guy's name more than twice or my partner behaved differently around coworkers, I suspected hidden agendas.

Past relationships emphasized my vigilance, as I had been dumped for someone else many times. I yearned for love and success, but lived with one foot out, dreading betrayal. When other men circled my partner, I exerted dominance around them in a myriad of ways. On one occasion, my partner mentioned a new coworker in a band, which led me to show up at her job and make my presence known.

However, my attempts to control and protect backfired. My paranoid behavior pushed my partner away and gave others a chance to treat her better. Unexpected gestures and invitations evoked paranoia and anxiety in me, but instead of being nicer, I pushed even harder. The obsession to prevent betrayal consumed me and holding my partner as a prime suspect proved to be a journey-ending mistake.

I transformed from a concerned partner to a paranoid one. My words turned to accusations, and our disagreements morphed into heated fights, resentment, and a painful separation. Living through the lens of my insecurities turned the person I valued most into an enemy, and I reaped what I sowed.

My jealousy had destroyed multiple relationships, but I attributed failures to others' flaws, not my own. The innermost fear of losing my partner pushed me to behave in counterintuitive ways, eventually leading to the moment I dreaded most.

A long, challenging year followed my first wife's departure. My dreams vanished, leaving a scar equal to the future moments I murdered. Jealousy hadn't protected me; instead, it shielded my belief in love and happiness despite evidence to the contrary.

From that moment on, I charged head-on against the dragon of jealousy. It took becoming conscious of my actions as they unfolded to change my inner dialogue on the spot. The voice of fear surfaced when I felt threatened, but I talked myself down by remind myself where that approach had taken me, and the price of fear. If I wanted to defeat this beast once and for all, I had to find a valid reason to act in the opposite fashion.

In subsequent relationships, I worked diligently to overcome jealousy by supporting my partners in their choices. I struggled with anxiety but persevered, finding joy in their happiness. While many situations triggered deeply ingrained reactions, I opted for a new path;

healing myself to avoid bleeding on the ones who didn't cut me.

Diving into past trauma revealed the roots of my jealousy, including my biological father's abandonment. My (step)dad's differences between my brother and I, my first girlfriend's infidelity, getting replaced at work without warning, two divorces, etc. The fear of losing what or who I loved to others better than me had tormented since childhood, stripping me of my self-worth. But when I compared the life I had built for myself, versus the shadows of dragons past; I understood that I had been good enough all-along, and that I only experienced the results of my choices.

Understanding that my behavior stemmed from feelings of unworthiness allowed me to heal. I learned that control led to pain, and that jealousy meant I had inner work to do. By focusing on building self-confidence and trust, I found peace and the freedom to give my best without expectations. The seed of jealousy had once spelled destruction, but by embracing trust and self-improvement, I discovered a path toward healthier connections.

Healing from old trauma allowed me to behave better, creating an atmosphere of trust and support. I understood that the best shot I got is to be the best self I can and allow the rest to unfold in its own accord. And it also allowed me to become the person I wanted to find; the one that understands that sharing our path is our choice, and that allowing your partner to experience life without constrains is a precious gift.

XXIX.

Warrior's Repose: The Healing Power of Regret

"The first to apologize is the bravest. The first to forgive is the strongest. The first to forget is the happiest." – Unknown

---

Growing up, my dad's perspective of apologies filled me with resentment, compelling me to repent for trivial things and punishing me if I resisted. Whether it was for quarreling with my brother, earning less-than-perfect grades, or failing to respond to him, apologizing became a form of torture. My childhood ingrained in me a fear of guilt and insufficiency, teaching me that humiliation cut deeper than physical pain.

As a kid, I was enchanted by G.I. Joe, Rambo, and Batman. On my 8th birthday, my dad gifted me a random action figure, while my younger brother received my favorite G.I. Joe character. My joy vanished in disappointment as I saw my dream toy in my brother's hand on my special day.

Throughout the day, my brother taunted me with his gift, mocking mine. Once I'd had enough, I retaliated. In an instant, my dad punished me and forced me to apologize, leaving me with a chilling warning.

As I grew older, my rebellion against authority intensified, fueled by resentment and pain. Apologies morphed into a perceived sign of weakness, a tool that could be used to hurt me. I had also grown angrier, power I used to defend myself and my new perspectives.

The challenge became evident when I got fired from a job for standing my ground. Although bummed for losing my source of income, I felt a sense of power wash over me. For the first time in my life, I had refused to bow down for a perceived benefit (or to avoid a fear) and realized that falling down didn't hurt as hard.

From then on, I tested the boundaries of my confidence by going further each time. Within a few years, my confident facade had morphed into unapologetic misbehavior, and my track record of failed jobs and relationships proved it. My refusal to apologize offered no emotional refuge, and getting divorced the second time underscored the need for change. I realized that I had trapped myself in a destructive cycle, choosing isolation over humility and vulnerability.

During my third engagement, I began to recognize the healing power of apologies. Through the lens of love, self-reflection, and the experience of single parenting, I understood that apologizing was not about conceding defeat but recognizing our shared human vulnerability. I discovered that sincere apologies could heal wounds, transforming them into a symbol of strength rather than weakness.

One day, I stumbled on Maya Angelou's "People don't remember how late you worked or how much you made, just how you made them feel" quote, and it struck me like a thunderbolt. Many of us chase financial status and material success, believing we do it for others' good, and I certainly had. Beneath that fruitless pursuit, however, I sought an emotional connection and self-worth that resonated deeper than any material gain.

Although I was considered a failure by society's standards; divorced twice by 36, single father of two, unemployed and bankrupt, I realized that I had the power to enrich my loved ones' lives right at my fingertips. Shoving my wisdom down their throats had been unnecessary; what mattered was recognizing our shared emotional nature and prioritizing their feelings over my own.

Facing my past and acknowledging my fears, I made a deliberate choice to become the father and partner I wanted to be, despite my screaming ego. I saw my pain reflected in others and chose to embrace it, learning new paths toward healing. Apologizing evolved into a conscious act of love, a way to mend wounds, foster trust, and nurture compassion.

However, a true challenge to my newfound understanding tested my beliefs, plunging me into an unexpected situation. As the turmoil of my second divorce subsided, I recognized my role in the breakdown of my marriage. My actions were a product of my upbringing, and resentment welled up against my father for not seeking better ways to raise me, ways I had diligently pursued for my children's well-being.

My attitude shifted, and I began treating him with disdain and contempt. In my mind, he had become a shadow, and I felt no obligation to heed his demands or conflicting guidance. Years of suppressed anger began to surface, and my behavior towards him unveiled my deepest resentment.

Yet, within a few short weeks, hate began to fester in my heart. Punishing my father for long-past deeds brought no solace; instead, it uncovered more reasons for regret. I learned that there's a balance in all things, and to find inner peace, I had to see the positive aspect of this situation.

Reflecting on my past, I understood that my father's stern methods had prepared me for life's trials. His guidance allowed me to weather unexpected challenges, and the early punishments of childhood saved me from bigger ones down the road. Thanks to my increased ability to endure pain, failure, and change, I found hidden blessings in uncertainty and order amid chaos.

The ugly face of pain and resentment had an equally beautiful counterpart. Having spared no criticism for my dad's mistakes, I recognized the responsibility to commend him for his strengths.

Once that realization hit me, I called him. We talked for a while, and I shared with him my newfound perspective. I apologized for being rude, hurtful and demeaning, and thanked him for teaching me all the right things. As a kid, I dreamed of going through the warrior's arduous training before the final battle, and my dad had given me no less.

The ensuing relief and peace were profound, and I knew I had discovered the path to authentic connection and self-awareness. My father seemed to shed an unseen weight, brought to tears as I expressed my gratitude and sought forgiveness for my actions. A transformative shift occurred within me, rejuvenating our bond on a foundation of mutual respect and heartfelt love.

This newfound ability to see beauty in situations I once resented opened my eyes to the incredible power of apology. With just a few sincere words, I healed years of bitterness, guilt, and pain. I now possessed a tool to heal those I had wronged, shedding the burden of self-reproach for not having known better.

In the realms of romance and parenting, apologizing became a means of recognizing and taking responsibility for actions that hurt others. It evolved into a commitment to repentance and a pledge not to repeat those mistakes. Owning up to my errors, I felt like I had found the invisible big bang of self-awareness that unveiled a universe of growth, fulfillment, and inner peace.

XXX.

Sparring with Shadows: The Illusion of Relationship Combat

"An eye for an eye only ends up making the whole world blind."
– Mahatma Gandhi

———————

Every romantic relationship I ventured into was riddled with conflicts, misunderstandings, and disagreements. These arguments bewildered me. Despite my efforts to craft solutions that satisfied both sides, I often found myself offending my partner and wallowing in frustration.

Navigating the aftermath of these arguments became an obsession for me. Facing a disagreement, I tried various approaches—different angles, ways of phrasing, and solutions to problems. But instead of finding common ground, my techniques only fueled frustration, leading my partners to react in unexpected ways.

Through two failed marriages, I learned that the sting of resentment and regret lingered long after arguments ended. I realized that mere listening or temperance wasn't enough; I needed to understand how our conflicts began, evolved, and how we could find resolution. Couples therapy, books and some courses had helped, but I continued to wrestle with this issue for some time.

The answer appeared in an unexpected place. During a Daito-ryu practice, the sensei explained the dojo's rules and combat etiquette to new students. We learned to fight and defend ourselves, but above all, we were taught to protect and care for one another. Growth could only be derived from proper practice, and that meant knowing — and respecting — our partners' limits. I knew first-hand the value of this guideline; during a Krav-Maga practice session, my sparring partner went too far and dislocated my shoulder.

A revelation occurred: the same principle could be applied to arguments. While no one suffered physically in our verbal sparring, handling our conversations the wrong way hurt each other past our emotional limits. The unexpected emotional blows – in both directions – were a result of not knowing our arguing styles. Although I had recognized patterns in our arguments before, I had failed to understand how they intertwined.

In conflict, I swung between being a fierce advocate for my viewpoint or a disengaged spectator. My peace of mind took precedence, often at the cost of resolution, and many of my relationships. I'd argue until my partner's frustration became apparent, then I'd disengage, retreating into myself to avoid escalation.

My detachment, though, distanced us emotionally, leading to inevitable breakups.

After two decades of failed relationships, a painful truth hit me: my arguing style manifested my deepest fears, especially the terror of abandonment. Every one of my reactions was founded on avoiding emotional disdain but had only expedited my passage there. I faced a choice between being right or finding peace.

It was a heated argument with my fiancée that crystallized the dynamics of our arguing styles. Trapped in my habitual emotions, I lay on the couch wrestling with frustration after the fight. But aware of my thought pattern, and determined to find a solution, I researched arguing styles to overcome this invisible barrier.

I found that each personality type handles stress uniquely, with many responses being unconscious. My arguing style was detachment; hers was a need for validation and reassurance. My natural reactions often worsened our emotional turmoil, responding in the opposite way she needed me to.

The path became clear: To find peace at the end of a fight, I had to overcome emotional detachment. Although I felt safe in my own emotional fortress, I also tortured myself to no end. To free myself, I needed to support and comfort my partner, regardless of the validity of my point. I had to overcome my ego's weaknesses and act in our relationship's best interest, strengthening rather than weakening our bond.

Facing the unknown territory of vulnerability, I apologized and reassured her. Besides replaying the fight in my mind to find what she had done wrong, I also looked at my own actions, understood how they affected her, and apologized for them.

My partner's eyes opened wide, and she stared sobbing. Her apology followed, explaining that work had been extra demanding that week, her mom had been sick, and she had hit an emotional wall, driving her to overreact with me. The fear of rejection fell off my chest, replaced by the peace and relief I dreamed of after a fight. In that moment I realized that the seemingly invincible beast had been a paper dragon, exaggerated by my ego's shortsightedness.

By uncovering, and managing, our arguing patterns, we found peace and understanding. Just like in martial arts, I couldn't spar properly without knowing our fighting styles. We became aware of our limits, resolved our differences, and recognized the value of resolution over lingering resentment.

With time and practice, I shed my combative style and learned to ask for feedback first. The process transformed not just my relationships but my entire approach to conflict and understanding.

We became a help against ourselves, much like the master at the dojo pushed our limits to help our growth.

We now protect each other's emotional state over any issues or opinions, prioritizing our relationship over the fears of our past. Finding each other at the end of an argument is not just a resolution — it's a reaffirmation of our commitment. We've learned to spar with words, not to wound, but to strengthen, guided by the wisdom that recognizing our unique fighting styles is the key to understanding and love.

XXXI.

Fool's Gold: Uncovering a Real Treasure

"The happiness of your life depends upon the quality of your thoughts."
– Marcus Aurelius

———————————————

In the realm of perception and thoughts, there's a belief that the material world is a manifestation of our ideas, brought to life by the work of our actions. By the time I turned 22, I experienced what I had — thus far — considered a mystical claim. I tripled my income and leased a sports car within three months. My life resembled the dream I had as a young immigrant; fancy car, nice clothes, married to someone I was in love with, and a big nod from those around me.

But at that same time, the other side of me worked overtime, reminding me that it wasn't enough yet. I began focusing of trivial pursuits, the goals that others deemed worthy of achieving. Designer clothes, exotic cars and expensive dinners fed my need for approval, but also my ego.

My self-centered behavior, orbiting material possessions, led me to value my achievements over the person I shared my life with, and I eventually lost her. The thrill of possessions disappeared, leaving me in agony and driving me to seek something more profound.

After my divorce, finding love seemed like an insurmountable task. Despite the number of dates I went on, I could not tap into that feeling again. I ended dates for trivial issues, left partners before they left me, and often found reasons to not go on. Disenchanted by the reality of dating, I spent time revisiting my needs and desires. I reassessed my expectations, perceived needs, and willingness to work with others' shortcomings.

To accomplish my goal, I accepted dates with people I, for whatever reason, wouldn't consider as potential mates. At first, I tried with accepting others for who they are, or at least tolerating them. If their habits or traits bothered me, I looked for ways to overcome my judging nature, and justified sticking together. That approach led me to become resentful, harboring negative thoughts until they manifested in breakups.

I then resorted to sharing my opinion and improvement suggestions. If I perceived that a partner could do something better, I was sure to let them know. In my mind, I tried my best to make things work, but every relationship seemed destined to fail. How could it be that I found a deal-breaker with everyone I encountered? It took me years to uncover the answer.

I remember my first car, a 1993 Chevy Cavalier. For the first two years in the U.S., I walked or took public transportation to jobs and points of interest. I spent hours traveling daily, time I spent learning and dreaming about the freedoms of a car.

One day, my dream came true, and my parents gifted me the Cavalier after they purchased a minivan. Getting this car meant pursuing my dream as a motocross racer, better jobs, and — maybe — finding love.

My new (to me) car got adorned with seat covers and fresheners, and any personal touches I could afford. For months, I explored at my leisure. I started racing motocross, worked at a guitar store, and dated someone. The Cavalier had become the keys to freedom until someone close to me ridiculed it. The fuzzy seat covers, and shiny wheel-caps were clearly distasteful, and who knows how many people had laughed at me behind my back.

It took buying and selling 15 cars over the years to realize that my emotional state derived from what I perceived the car meant to me, and not the actual car itself. The rush of getting a new car seemed to be the same every time, yet the price tag and burden for bigger-and-better became greater in every transaction.

Unknowingly, this pattern extended into my relationships. I idealized potential partners in the first few dates, grew disenchanted, and pointed fingers at them for no longer having what we had before. I fixated on shortcomings rather than appreciating the positives, becoming a nagging nightmare. Friendships, relationships, and even two marriages fell apart before I considered another way.

Previously, I'd judged and compared partners to my mind's ideal version. But this led to defensiveness and accusations. If I voiced a complaint, partners defended themselves with counterattacks. Stonewalling made me a coward; holding my ground escalated the fight. This was a path I knew well yet could not find a way out of.

But one thing had become clear; no matter what I wanted or expected, it never seemed to be enough. Was a working relationship an impossible goal? Just like my car conundrum, it had been and was going to be if I kept emphasizing what I lacked over the many beautiful things I had access to.

If my thoughts created my reality, my sour relationships and emotional state directly reflected my innermost fears. Focusing on what I didn't get or had lost only increased its importance in my eyes, becoming a beam that blinded my choices.

From that moment on, I made a conscious choice to value what my loved ones meant for me. I cherished the magical moments we shared, the many beautiful chords they plugged into my life symphony, and the embrace of love I had sought. I chose to express gratitude instead of complaints, and my reality flourished with the product of my thoughts.

Life began to change, and my emotional state brightened each day I recognized the beauty in my life and relationship. Instead of cars and material achievement, I decided to test a timeless principle in my love relationships, and the results proved undeniable.

Stumbling upon the joy and fulfillment of adopting a love bias, that is, valuing my partners' real attributes and personality over my expectations, has been a gift that freed me from the chains of suffering. To realize that it had been my perspective, and not others, that needed adjustment, evoked in me the peace of knowing that I could find everything I wanted within myself, and that the relationship I had always dreamed of wasn't only possible, but also sustainable. Like Marcus Aurelius' timeless wisdom at the beginning of this chapter, I only had to change my lens to find what I wanted.

Falling in love is a decision, an ongoing process. Love and hate are degrees of the same emotional spectrum, and by knowing where to look, we can experience what we yearn for most. I found it required less effort to remember our first kiss in detail than to wrestle with the many imaginary hopeless scenarios that result from negative thinking.

By aligning my thoughts and actions, I went from hopelessness to recognizing the value in others, especially those who stood by me despite my flaws. The treasure I had sought for decades hid beneath my own feet, and everything else that had disappeared, simply fool's gold.

XXXII.

Taming the Serpent of Loss: Embracing Today's Treasures

"Look to this day for it is life, the very life of life." - Sanskrit Proverb

---

Ever since my family moved from my grandparents, I've lived a nomadic life, inhabiting over 35 homes across countries and continents. Driven by my father's pursuit of a better life, I've said goodbye to friends, family, and even pets, more times than I care to count. By 17, I had moved thirteen times, with loss and change as my only constants.

After I graduated high school, my father and I migrated to the United States, fleeing Argentina's financial crisis. My future as a systems analyst and full-ride scholarship dissolved as I packed a carry-on for this new adventure. Days after arriving in New Jersey, I got my first job washing dishes at a restaurant, working foot-blistering shifts to help rebuild our lives.

About a year after moving, I found work at a mall and began to connect with others, feeling the thrill of social interaction. I even fell in love, but my lack of confidence, experience, and a car held me prisoner of my insecurities. The girl I liked was out of my league, and she was dating someone else.

We worked together for a year, until I lost my job along with the courage to confess my feelings. A few weeks later I got a job at a nearby jewelry store in the same mall. When she discovered where I worked, she found and kissed me, turning my dream into reality. My bliss was short-lived, however, when she left me for someone else a few months later.

Although I had endured going from riches to rags, moving to different countries and sacrificing my career for basic jobs, being left for someone else was a different type of beast. The physical hurt of being blindsided led to self-doubt, anger, and desperate pleads for reconciliation. I mourned for weeks, torturing myself with thoughts of what I could have done differently. To cope with my feeling of unworthiness, I sought relief in motocross, playing guitar in a heavy metal band, and earning more money.

At 22, after various dates and pursuits, I fell in love again. Despite seeking validation in extreme sports, music, and social media, they were all dead-end alleys. In love and with a chance at a happily-ever-after, we got married. That union dissolved a year later, along with cars, apartment, and my desire to chase other dreams. Being divorced at such a young age flipped my world – and self-perception – upside down.

Alone once again, I faced the agony of losing someone I loved, devoid of understanding. Was I truly that flawed? I began to suspect that relationships weren't meant to last, and my desperate but futile attempts solidified this belief. Hopelessness washed over me, and I lost the desire to go on.

The emotional hell I lived in became insufferable, forcing me to find answers. Solitude had helped me heal, but also built a fortress of fear around me, terrified of making the same mistakes. I also knew, somehow, that there had to be an answer for my dilemma. Otherwise, another relationship would be futile, and a life of loneliness guaranteed.

Soon after my divorce I lost my grandfather. My family moved to South America, and I lost my job at the car dealership. Within weeks, the reality I once enjoyed had become a nightmare. Sitting in my empty living room, I realized everything I had worked for, everyone I knew, and everything I had sacrificed, had been for nothing.

A deep sense of sadness possessed me, leading me to question my existence and my reasons to live. Instead of allowing myself to wither inside, I sold what I had left and vagabonded the world. Love found me again, leading to another marriage and a child. But seven years later, disaster struck again.

Much like in previous relationships, our efforts to overcome obstacles had become ammunition against each other. My heart wept; years of sacrifice to build a family only to see it turn to sand in my own hands. This third blow left me stripped of everything — my job, business, home, family; even my will to live. This time I had plunged to the bottom of the abyss.

After enduring my second divorce, along with unemployment, living in my car, and the COVID-19 pandemic, I relinquished my grip on life. I had rebuilt myself three times, only to stumble and fall again. I felt defeated, without desire to build, discover or pursue anything else.

But fatherhood was the slap that awakened me. After the divorce, I cared for my two kids full time, learning the ropes of single parenting. The pressures of life drowned me, and eventually my negative emotional state poured into everyday life. Once I realized my behavior generated negative emotions on those around me, I became aware of how low I had fallen. I resolved to get back up, and to become the person my children deserved, not the failure I deemed myself to be.

I accepted life's transient nature based on its inevitable cycles, vowing to make every moment the best I could. No amount of pressure, juggling, or success had prevented anyone from leaving me, but by creating for others the emotional home I yearned for, I would at least have peace if they chose to. By shifting my focus from fear to opportunity, I began perceiving each day as a chance to bestow joy, love, and unity upon others and myself.

The fear of losing loved ones – and things – eventually disappeared, replaced by the opportunity to create magical moments whenever I could. In the past, I spent countless hours dreading the day I no longer enjoyed someone's company. Now, I cherish the time and space we have together while we have it, understanding the inevitability of change.

In the words of Alfred Lord Tennyson, "It's better to have loved and lost than never to have loved at all." I now agree, realizing that the Universe's gifts to us are our talents and loved ones; our gifts to the Universe are what we do with them.

XXXIII.

From the Valley of Shadows, to the Mountain of Light: Conquering the Last Dragon

"Know Thyself." – Ancient Greek Aphorism

A year had passed since my fiancé, the children, our dogs, and I moved in together with dreams of marriage and a new home. We had been dating for nearly three years, sharing our expenses and responsibilities. On our second year in the new home, my company crumbled, pushing me to find work or at least a source of income. But as months went by without a job or money, those dreams — and our relationship — began to dwindle.

The process to find help humbled my most stubborn misconceptions. Over 100 job applications without results forced me to face the truth of my real abilities, masked under feigned competence. Once I ran out of money and things to sell, my fiancé's grace kept us going, but the shame became unbearable.

The dread of financial collapse and a shortage of options drowned me. I felt insufficient, but my partner remained strong, without complaint. Soon, though, cracks appeared in our relationship. A few months without a penny from me weighed on her, emotions that translated to other areas of life. To ease the burden, I sold my car and gave her the money to cover expenses.

The strain began to take its toll. The love and warmth between us waned with each emotional bruise, replaced by tension and arguments. Each day seemed darker, and hope began to fade. My job search had been fruitless, my credit cards maxed out, and I had run out of things to sell. But I continued to seek, write, learn, and believe in a brighter tomorrow.

By the fourth month, our fights escalated to levels I hadn't seen since my second divorce. I relived a painful past and drowned in the fear of a future where my children suffered due to my actions. The pain of my past actions and shortsightedness weighed me down; the fear of causing my kids the emotional harm, loss, or suffering I had endured as a child terrified me.

Overcoming my first marriage had broken — but also toughened — me; surviving the second divorce had brought me to my knees. But now, this third blow had me face down on the ground. One late night, after another futile attempt to make money online, I went to bed, only for the fight to reignite.

I sat on the bed and made small talk to ease the tension. However, she seemed to have been waiting for this moment, unleashing an explosion of anger and frustration that caught me by surprise. Within minutes, I heard the most hurtful things yet; she broke up with me and announced her plans to move out. The fear I felt as a child, being kicked out of my house at 8, returned, amplified by the realization that my failures had led me here.

Years of searching for love, purpose, and peace had left me shattered. I had changed my ways, opened businesses, pursued professional dreams, and even learned to live with nothing but my sense of self-worth. But I found myself drowning deeper than before.

The storm of despair clouded my mind. I had done my very best, day in and day out, to end up in the same place. This time, however, it was worse than ever, and my children could suffer again because of me. This situation pushed me to consider the unthinkable: leaving my children with money from my life insurance policy. The unknown of the afterlife seemed a better option than the known failures of my existence. Perhaps my life wasn't a waste after all; easing my emotional torment and leaving my children and partner (or ex-wife) with a home was more than I had been able to do anyways.

But in that moment of despair and surrendering, the light of dawn broke the darkest night, and understanding flooded in. My purpose became clear: to share with my children the wisdom that I had painfully acquired. No amount of money, homes, or inheritance could spare them from the traps of life, but my foolish journey could serve as a map to avoid painful failures. I could guide them away from my mistakes, teaching them about resilience, dreams, and the promise of a new dawn.

I resolved to become a better writer and a better person, to share my golden nuggets of wisdom. Even in my darkest hour, I recognized the importance of those around me and my responsibility to share my experience for their benefit.

Mentally back on the couch, I picked myself up, washed my face, and faced the last dragon in the kingdom. I went back to my partner, expressed my love and understanding, and let her know she was free to follow her dreams. I had resolved to be the emotional home I wanted, for those I loved, and that meant putting my needs — and fears — aside in favor of what my partner desired. To love is to let free.

Her response surprised me. She confessed that her anger was rooted in her fears of abandonment. She had confused my reserved approach to marriage with a lack of commitment and sought certainty by planning what's next. Sharing my honest and vulnerable emotions gave her all the reassurance she needed, and in exchange, the fears that pushed us apart disappeared.

In the months that followed, our lives transformed. My children flourished, relationships healed, and I began coaching. I continued to learn, teach, grow, and enjoy the journey. Instead of threats, the unknown now offers opportunities, and everyday events seem to happen for us, not against. The foundation of our relationship became rock solid, allowing us to thrive in other life endeavors.

The last battle in my heart freed me from fear, pain, and suffering. Conquering my fears armed me with the sword of knowledge and led me to the oasis of love, peace, and fulfillment I sought my entire life.

Through years of tribulation and triumph, I've come to understand the value of experience, the importance of sharing those lessons, and the realization that each of us carries the key to unlocking our innermost treasure. This book is not merely a recounting of my journey; it's an offering and tribute to you, dear reader.

I wrote these pages with you in mind, hoping that my experiences help you avoid the traps and pitfalls that once ensnared me. Every hardship endured, every lesson learned, and every word penned is aimed at guiding you toward a better path, or at least away from pain and suffering.

My unconventional path led me through dark nights and bright days, from despair to love, from confusion to purpose, and from conflict to peace. And I want you to know that you, too, can find the utopian emotional state we all seek.

If I could find my way through the maze of life, so can you. If I could rise from the ashes of defeat, so can you. If I could discover love, purpose, and peace, so can you.

Your journey may be different, filled with unique challenges and joys, but the destination remains the same. It's a place within you, where dreams become reality, where love blossoms, and where purpose and peace are not just distant ideals but a living, breathing part of your existence.

I hope that my words serve as a compass, guiding you through your own trials, helping you navigate the complex terrain of life, and leading you to a place of fulfillment and happiness.

Remember, dear warrior, this book was forged from my deepest pains and highest triumphs, all for you. May it light your way, may it fortify your resolve, and may it help you find your own unconventional path to love, purpose, and peace.

Expose yourself to your deepest fear; after that, fear has no power, and the fear of freedom shrinks and vanishes. You are free." - Jim Morrison

Made in the USA
Middletown, DE
25 September 2023

39366321R00094